RYAN CH

UNWANTED

A WAY TO FORGIVE
THOSE WHO NEVER DESERVE IT

RC Publishing

TABLE OF CONTENTS

I.

FOREWORD

IF YOU ARE a person constantly smiling, proclaiming the blessings life has brought you, and are truly happy, this work is not for you. I am trying to reach a very specific person to tell him/her three things: you're not alone, it's not your fault, and you too can find peace.

Despite my uprbringing, I was a two-time high school speech and debate national qualifier. I went to college on a full academic scholarship. I got a scholarship to attend law school (yes, they do give those out). I've been appointed by the governor of a state to sit on a university wide board of directors. I have written a nationwide speech and debate manual for charity. I used to run marathons. I had a high school speech and debate coach who was like a father to me and an Aunt who would take a bullet for me. Not to mention all my friends. I have more tennis and debate trophies than I could shake a stick at. I've had some big blessings in life. This book isn't about any of that.

This book is for anyone who is hurting and who has never forgiven (or even thought about forgiving) their offenders. This book is for the woman who was raped, the boy who was sexually abused by a family member, the spouse who caught their life partner in bed with another lover, and the child who just could not please his/her parents no matter how many trophies the kid brought home. This is for those who hurt. This book may be for you, and it definitely was for me.

In this book, I will tell you my story. Unapologetically raw and real. I will identify all of those who wronged me in a graphic way. I will detail every single attempt I made to forgive those who wronged me. And then I will tell you what finally worked for me.

I am not saying I have the solution for you. Trust me. I read numerous so-called "self-help" books and found them not remotely helpful despite bold forewords that prophesied I would be healed if I followed the author's advice. I have tried every program, therapist, group help, a brief stint in A.A. (although I wasn't an alcoholic), pastors' messages, bible stories, and confessions to many dear friends. I tried writing letters and that only brought temporary relief. None of these methods were overly helpful. At most, they provided temporary relief.

If my words have resonated with you so far, then please turn the page and keep reading. It's a quick read. Although brief, I want to warn you that some of this material may be difficult to digest. There is no right or wrong way to approach this stuff. You may need to read this work, "in chunks." Do whatever works for you.

This book has three parts: My Story, The Solution, and Peace. You may be tempted to just read my story. I encourage you to read on. It may be the best decision you have ever made.

I'm not a psychologist. I'm a lawyer, adjunct professor at a local community college, tennis player, and CrossFit° athlete. Most importantly, I am a person who has been abused in every way you could probably imagine (and in a few ways I pray you probably can't.).

While this book contains references to Christianity, it is a secular piece. Whatever your faith beliefs or lack thereof, I am going to provide you with what worked for me. I hope it works for you, too.

Many of the individuals mentioned in this book are still alive. Many of the events described in this book would expose them to serious criminal liability. Wherever possible, I have concealed their identities for their own sake.

My inspiration for putting this book together came from three sources. The first was internal. I had all this stuff swimming around in my head that was impacting literally everything I did. The second was from my college class. I teach Introduction to Public Speaking at a local community college. During the final one semester, many students chose to address a topic regarding mental health care in the United States. The statistics I heard were shocking. What surprised me even more were the personal stories these students shared. It was very disturbing information. Combined with my own past, I knew something needed to be done. The third source of inspiration was from one of my dearest friends in life, Big T. Big T instructed me that I had to forgive my father and that forgiveness was the only way out. Big T was right.

All the stories in this book are true. They all happened. To me. When most people meet me, they are usually shocked to hear all the horrific parts of my past. But I assure you these are 100% true. Growing up, I was a good actor; I hid well.

I hope this book does for you what it did for me. I was 32 years old when this book was written. I wasted three decades of my years on this Earth angry, shattered, and alone. It doesn't have to be this way. There's hope. For you.

And one last thing. Just trust me. If I can make it, you can too.

II.

PART ONE: MY STORY

A. I WAS 22

I was 22 years old when I found out. I vividly remember the revelation.

I was a first-year law student visiting my then girlfriend's apartment in Bartlesville, Oklahoma. Daylight savings time had more than set in so even though it was around 7:00 PM, it was very dark out. The weather was cool and mild on that December day.

Standing at the bottom of the stairs, I was talking on a very early generation of the iPhone to my one family member I still communicate with: Aunt Mary. She was always been there for me. Even though we have not always gotten along, she's always loved me.

I was hurting. Bad. I could not figure out why my mother had not called me but twice that semester. I could not figure out why my father was such an ass all the time. Then, she told me.

I remember immediately feeling a very strong gut reaction to what she said. Mentally, I went somewhere else. I'm not really sure why. But when I processed the words, my world became much clearer, and much darker.

My mother tried to conceive numerous times and failed. I am supposed to have a brother a year older than my current brother and a sister a year older than me. Due to late-term miscarriages, my eldest brother and sister did not make it through pregnancy. This very negatively damaged an already strained marriage. My father then decided he did not want to proceed with another attempt at having another child. My mother disagreed. She then lied to my father about being on birth control. I was the result.

It made perfect sense to me once I found out. It explains all the violence, abuse, emotional damage, and all the horrific scars that follow.

I am now going to take you through the rest my story. You need to understand that what follows in the pages to come are tales of some very disturbing events. When this book was in its early stages, I asked several of my closest friends to read and opine their thoughts. One of my friends told me she teared up as she read it. Another told me she had to read it in parts as it was too much to take in at once. Another described it as, "disturbing." You have been forewarned.

If any of this resonates with you, keep reading.

B. My Father

i. *A Disturbing Start to Life*

By far my gravest offender in life to date is my dad. I struggled to even write the word "Dad" as I stopped referring to my biological father by that title many moons ago. But biologically, we are forever intertwined.

I never met my grandfather on my dad's side of the family. He died of a massive heart attack at the age of 57 years old in 1987, the year I was born. From what I understand, he had a very disturbed start to life. Apparently, my great grandfather and great grandmother gave life to my grandfather but had zero interest in being parents. One day, they drove to Neosho, Missouri (my hometown), to meet with Uncle Gus and Aunt Gusta. These two individuals were referred to as "aunt" and "uncle" but I do not know if there is a true blood relation. I do not know how Uncle Gus and Aunt Gusta were related to my grandfather, but I do know they could not have children and were exhilarated to have a child. Even though the child wasn't "theirs."

You would think that a child having another couple take him in would be thankful. I know I would have been! But that sense of abandonment very seriously scarred my grandfather, transforming a once happy person into a full-blown alcoholic. It is my understanding that my grandfather got drunk one night and tried to kill my dad, a then 14-year-old boy. I don't think my dad ever recovered from that event. Honestly, I struggle to see how someone could without considerable therapy and perhaps this book.

I was later told that my father asked Uncle Gus and Aunt Gusta to adopt him and Aunt Mary. They refused. I think that sense of rejection always stayed with him.

My dad is the hardest working person I have ever met. To most, that would seem like a compliment. It's not. He's a workaholic. He had three jobs my whole life growing up and never had any money. This was in part due to a serious porn addiction. While I never saw any of his films, it is my understanding he was into something called "Snuff." For those who don't know, "Snuff" is a type of porn where, after sex, the man murders the woman. There are various theories on whether this actually occurs or if it is somehow computer edited. I honestly do not know and am no less horrified by it. Whether or not this is true, my father had an ample collection of "Snuff" and viewed it routinely.

My dad works from the time he wakes up until the time he goes to sleep. Every day. He is an auto mechanic by trade and prefers to work alone. In fact, he very seriously does not want anyone's help. With anything. He was also an adjunct professor at a local community college where he taught a class in automotive technology. Finally, he was in the military. And he was a disgrace to the uniform. You will see why soon enough.

I struggled where to start with my dad because he is the most horrific monster of a human being I have ever met. What's most sad is that my dad has never, ever come close to facing any of his demons. I have a theory why. I am convinced if he ever came to grips with all the destruction he caused me and others, I am pretty sure he would kill himself.

Knowing and experiencing a portion of my life with my father has convinced me that demonic forces spiritually manifest in certain human beings. I have seen a look on my father's face that previously haunted me in my sleep. That raw, unchecked rage coupled with zero self-control is a violent force of nature that cannot be adequately described. Only experienced.

ii. Like Father, Like Son

Let's start with something I do not remember but was told about on that December night when I was 22.

When I was an infant, Aunt Mary, my dad, and my mom were outside at our home in Neosho. My father was working on something. He was using a garden hose when it became entangled. Because my father's response to every little inconvenience in life is losing his temper immediately, he yanked the hose as hard as he could. Apparently, I was seated in a stroller and the stroller was situated over the hose. The ripple effect of his violent tug caused the hose to hit the stroller and sent me flying in the air. Mind you the area where they were doing whatever it was they were doing was a concrete surface. I did not have a helmet on. My mother and Aunt Mary dove and caught me. I was saved only by the Grace of God. Now, I do not know nor do I believe that my father intentionally tried to kill me. But I do wonder if he set that moment up to see. I do not know if I will ever have the answer to that question.

iii. Dad & Dogs

For some reason, my father has never liked dogs. As an adult, it seems disturbing that a human would not enjoy the company of man's best friend. But I do not believe my father enjoys the company of anyone, not even himself.

When I was very young, I loved listening to rap music. Probably because my brother got me hooked on it. As a white kid growing up in the 90's in a small town in Missouri, of course I could easily relate to what my favorite rapper, Snoop Doggie Dogg, was saying in his songs.

My mother finally convinced my father to let us get a dog and we got a Chinese Pug. My brother and I named him Snoop after our favorite rapper. Snoop was a good dog.

I do not remember what Snoop did, which probably means he didn't do anything, but one night my father got very angry at Snoop. For those who have never had a Chinese Pug, they are very small dogs. Snoop was particularly small as I believe he was the runt of his litter. My father stood at the top of the stairs to our basement yelling and cussing at the dog. Snoop tried to get away but was unsuccessful. My father threw Snoop at a wall as hard as he could where the dog then shrieked in pain as he ricocheted off the wall and fell about six feet to the bottom of the stairs. It broke his back left leg. Honestly, I'm surprised it didn't kill him.

My dad then got annoyed as he had to spend money to take Snoop to the vet. I did not attend the appointment, but I've always wondered what the vet was told regarding the incident described above. I'm sure a lie of some sort was concocted.

It takes a truly screwed up human being to abuse an animal. And trust me when I say that my dad is truly screwed up.

iv. Shoving the Supervisor

One night my dad came home from work around 8:00 PM. This was odd as it was "early" (he usually got home around midnight or later). I do not remember what happened, but he started telling my mother that he might lose his job. Apparently, my father and his supervisor at work got into it (this routinely happened). This time, things got out of hand and my father shoved the supervisor against a locker in a locker room. He then cussed him out at the top of his lungs. After telling my mother this story, my father then left home and returned to work.

Thankfully for our family's sake, my father did not lose his job. My father's supervisor was a very kind, forgiving man who understood that my father had a nasty temper. I believe my father was written up but not terminated. Honestly, he probably should have been.

v. *Mommy Shhheeock*

One of my father's favorite go-to's is to identify something that annoys him and then make it infinitely worse by assigning some offensive nickname to it.

For whatever reason, my mother's health has never been great. She was never diagnosed with any immune disorders of which I'm aware. However, she routinely took sick days as she did not feel well. After processing the events I'm writing in this piece, I believe that her depression would sometimes get the better of her causing her to feel ill. You see, my mother has a very serious form of depression. Worse, it remains untreated for reasons that are still somewhat unclear to me.

My father believes that work is the most important thing in life. If you're happy, work. If you're mad, work. If you're sick, work. If you're healthy, work. Work. Work. Work. That was him. If you disagreed with him, or took time for yourself for whatever reason, you are lazy. Laziness, in his book, is a cardinal sin of the highest order.

At some point in my childhood, my father started calling my mother and his then-wife "Mommy Shhheeock." The word "shhheeock" was his way of saying "sick" but pronouncing it slightly differently. He was essentially mocking my mother's untreated depression.

One time I was on the phone with my dad and I said the word mom as I was describing a conversation we had. He immediately interrupted without apology and used one of his favorite sentences. "Mommy Shheeock! The name that'sh shynomoush with shicknesshh and illnesshh. Mommy Shheeock!"

He would call her this routinely. He would call her this to her face, when speaking with my brother and I about her, and even to what few friends he had. It made my mother cry. If he cared, it wasn't enough for him to cease and desist.

vi. Weed eaters

I have never met a person who had more difficulties with mowing the lawn than my father. We would jokingly tell other people that the neighbors would get out their lawn chairs and popcorn on a summer Sunday night to observe the spectacle that was my father attempting to start a weed eater.

Looking back, I believe my father struggled with weed eaters because he probably bought the cheapest one you could buy. When it comes to lawn equipment, I've learned as an adult that you get what you pay for.

One particular Sunday night the weed eater would not start, and my father's temper was particularly high. He finally gave up and grabbed his sledgehammer. My father's sledgehammer was his favorite "tool" to "fix" broken equipment. I can testify under oath with 100% certainty that my father's sledgehammer has never fixed any tool in the manner in which he used it.

My father beat the weed eater with the sledgehammer until it was in multiple pieces. He then put it back in the box and attempted to return it to Wal-Mart. It was not successfully returned.

vii. Broken Down June

My Grandma Norma June Childress, aka, "Grandma June," was a very sweet woman. Growing up, I'm told that she was not always the kindest person. It really wasn't her fault. She was bipolar and this was back when those who had a mental illness were "committed." She was not committed and therefore her manic bipolar went unchecked and untreated, producing some very erratic behavior. I do not know what my grandmother did to my father, but I gather that she was not always pleasant to him.

My grandmother had considerable health problems later in life. She had a weight problem, all kinds of mental health issues, and eventually acquired Alzheimer's that ultimately took her life.

While my grandmother was in the very early stages of Alzheimer's, she had considerable medical appointments. My father lived in the same town as her but genuinely hated doing anything but working. He would always complain about taking his mother to the doctor's appointments as he described his own mother as a "burden."

When complaining about his mother and all the appointments she required, he resorted to his favorite approach of assigning an offensive nickname. He constantly described his own mother as "Broken Down Juuuuuuune." If he had to take her to an appointment, he would always say he had to take "Broken Down June to the God-damned doctor."

Keep in mind this was the man's own mother.

viii. The Pedal Go-Cart

When I was very young, pedaled go-carts were released. My birthday was coming up and I saw one of these on commercial. I was immediately in love. Thankfully, my family purchased one for me for my birthday. I do not remember how old I was, but I remember being very young.

We traveled to Toys-R-Us to pick up the vehicle. I could hardly contain my excitement. The store clerk behind the pickup counter alerted my father that the go-cart was not assembled even though it should have been. Mind you I was very young, but the man behind the counter could not have been very old.

My father has zero patience for anyone or anything. When the man told him the bike was not ready, my father immediately lost his temper, raised his voice to the peak of his lungs, and started liberally cussing. "What do you F***ing mean the God damn thing isn't F***ing ready? This is horseshit!" The young man somehow held it together as my father was pounding his fists on the counter and cussing out a teenage boy.

Thankfully, the manager came over and calmly handled the situation. I left with the show model on the store floor.

My father never apologized to the teenage boy, the manager, or me for this outburst. In fact, on the way home, he laughed at how he cussed out the teenager as he thought it was funny.

ix. What Changed My Brother

I remember I was sitting at home on a Saturday night watching the movie Ghostbusters with my mom and dad. My dad loved to watch movies and that's what we routinely did as a family.

Suddenly, a police officer knocked on the door. He told us that my older brother and only sibling had been caught shoplifting at a store at the mall in Joplin, Missouri, and that he was being held in juvenile detention. I remember the car ride to Joplin very vividly. It was like watching water boil. The longer my father talked, the angrier he became. When we arrived at the detention center, my brother was genuinely shaking he was so scared. My father yelled. All the way home. When we got home, my mother kept me in the car while my father took my brother inside. I expected a spanking. I did not expect this.

I could still hear my father yelling as my mother and I looked down at the floorboard. I heard my father's belt slide through the loops. The next sound I heard I do not think I will adequately be able to describe.

I believe my father removed my brother's shirt, although I do not know this. I remember my father swinging the leather belt and making contact so loud I could hear the sound of leather slapping bare skin while sitting in a car with the doors closed outside my house. I looked up and saw my father's shadow. His arm was fully raised and shoulder fully extended. The momentum he generated from his swing was unreal. I believe he may have even jumped for extra force.

I do not remember what happened next. I remember eventually going inside and my brother was seated in the shower with the water running. He had his knees to his chest, his head between his legs, and his arms folded in front of his legs.

I was crying in my bedroom. My dad came in and said he didn't want to do what he did, but he had to. I disagree.

x. The Divorce

My parents got divorced when I was 10. I had a swing set outside where I would spend a great deal of time. To this day, I still love swinging. I used to love listening to my cd player and daydream. It was where I found peace as a kid. I remember being on the swing set when my mother walked outside with a note she had just written. She told me she was going to leave my father. I got upset more so because I was a worrier and wondered how we would make it financially. Remember, I was 10. I had to grow up as a kid. Quick.

When my mother told my father that she was leaving him, it got ugly in a hurry. Apparently, my mother charged up $20,000.00 in unsecured credit card debt and then filed for bankruptcy. Because they were married at the time, this meant the credit card companies could go after my dad. I estimate that my swing set was probably a good 30 yards from my house. I can still hear his voice, yelling at the top of his lungs towards my mother. "You useless f***ing bitch, you don't matter for shit!" There were lots of four-letter words peppered throughout statements of hate flying out of his mouth.

My brother went inside in an attempt to intervene. He was 15 at the time. Even though a younger man, my brother was about the same size as my dad. But there was nothing he could do against that level of unchecked rage.

You see, I have witnessed and experienced hatred in its purest, rawest, unchecked form in my father. I genuinely believe that kind of deep-seated disgust is demonic in nature and comes from below. I have no research to support this theory. And I cannot prove it. But watching my father behave convinced me of two things. One, he is not a good person. Two, I believe in demons because I've seen one: him.

A moment after my brother entered our house, I heard my father scream, "Get the F*** out of here! I don't want you to F***ing see this." What I saw next was truly horrifying. I saw my brother's body fly out the front door like someone tossed a garbage bag into the dumpster. I didn't think a human being could be thrown like that. I do not remember how he landed. But I remember him being very upset. Not surprisingly, his own father just treated him like a sack of garbage.

What follows next is even more disturbing. Keep in mind I was not in the room, but I could hear everything that was going on. And my aunt Mary happened to be there who later in life told me the details of what happened that day.

Taking a step back, we did not know there was a plan for my mother to get all of her and our stuff out of the house that weekend. My father was in the Army National Guard at the time. Part of his commitment was one weekend a month where he had to "Drill." I do not know what occurred at these drills, but I do know he had to be there from Friday at 6:00 PM and could not leave until Sunday at 6:00 PM. This gave my mother the perfect opportunity to escape. And she took it.

We spent that weekend with Aunt Mary because that's what we got to do as kids. Even though Aunt Mary lived 60 miles away in Springfield, Missouri, we would always go spend time with her. When she brought us back that weekend, my brother and I walked into an empty house. All our stuff was gone. We instantly froze. Later, my aunt told us we were in shock based on our physical and mental response to that situation.

My aunt then took us to Shoney's, one of the few decent restaurants in our hometown. On the way, she called my dad and had a private conversation with him. Keep in mind these are the days before car connectivity and cell phones. She was saying things we could hear, but I do not remember any of her words. She later told me that she was reporting to my dad what happened. My father was upset and met us at the restaurant, but he was too mad to speak. That state was not uncommon for him.

Back to the day the divorce was announced. After my father had gotten out what he thought was his last word, he started marching towards my mother. Thankfully, my aunt saw what was happening and intervened. She kicked my dad in the chest as hard as she could so my mother could lock herself in our basement and call the police. Later, my aunt told me it was the Lord's strength as my father could have easily over-powered her. I tend to agree.

I am convinced that if my father had gotten his hands on my mother, he would have killed her. He had abused her before, but this time was different. This time it was what mattered most to him: money.

About three minutes later, the police showed up. I still remember to this day the squad car arriving, lights and sirens blaring. It arrived in Fast-and-Furious style as the officer slammed on the brakes and skid sideways in front of our house.

The police officer rushed into the house with his gun drawn and told my father to leave. He did. But "leaving" really does not describe what was being played out before my eyes. He drove a Ford Ranger that was a manual transmission. He spun his tires halfway up a hill and was probably doing about 50 miles per hour before he shifted it into second gear. The speed limit on our street was 25.

The police interviewed me, my brother, my mother, and my aunt. My aunt and mother fought. Probably because my aunt wondered why in the world my mother would take all our stuff and not tell anyone she was going to do it. That was a very foolish decision on my mother's part. I was crying uncontrollably. I remember we had a trampoline and I was slamming my fists on it shouting, "Why? Why? Why?" I remember all the attention was on my brother, which was the usual case. I think that is the first time I felt truly alone.

Unknown to me, Aunt Mary drove to my then-teacher's home. She confessed to Mrs. McClintock, who was like a communal mother to my squad, everything she had just witnessed. The next day, Mr. Peterson, my middle school counselor, came and got me out of class. He had a chocolate milk with him. I sat down and told him what happened. He looked truly disgusted and very disturbed by the words flowing out of my mouth. I can still picture his face as I write these words.

xi. How It All Started

From there, things got perpetually worse. My mother started dating the second of many losers in her life. My first stepfather (deceased) was an abusive, violent alcoholic. He abused my mother. Later, after he and my mother divorced, he was involved in a very terrible car accident and died. A sixteen-year-old in a Cadillac Escalade who I believe was texting while drive swerved into his lane and caused him to lose control. He was driving a company dump truck that landed on top of him and crushed him. He had a very tragic end to life. Thankfully, the law firm that I was working for at the time represented my former stepfamily and was able to obtain a substantial sum of money on their behalf. That was good. They deserved it after suffering such a tragic loss.

My mother moved into a very small apartment on the other end of town after she and my father divorced. I moved in with my mother for about a year. For some strange reason, I never slept in my bedroom. I always slept on the couch. My stepfather routinely stayed over as he was "building" his house. He started building a home on some property his mother owned. His house was a perpetual work in progress. It was really just one room that had a toilet in it. My stepbrothers and I would stay up there when we eventually moved onto his property. It was novel as a child, but very sad as an adult.

My dad, brother, mother, and I took a vacation to Galveston, Texas. We stayed in this amazing hotel called Port Royal that was later destroyed by a hurricane. We only got to stay one night as we discovered the hotel after we arrived and already had reservations at another place. This place was immaculate. It had three waterfall pools that all flowed into one another. We swore we wanted to go back there one day. And we did! We stayed there for about four days before my dad decided he wanted to come back home because he missed working. The second time, it was just my dad, brother, and me.

We decided we wanted to return one more time. We made plans to go that summer after my fifth-grade year. You can imagine how excited my brother and I were. Two kids about to return to their favorite vacation destination of all time.

But we never got to go back. My mother recently took my father back to court to obtain additional child support on my "behalf." This was the days before income guidelines that most states have now adopted and parents could then agree to "reduced" amounts. Well, according to the laws at the time, my father was underpaying by about $100.00 a month. Now granted, I understand now that $100.00 is not very much money to him. But it was the principle of the thing to my father. Even though he was without the principles of even a decent person, he sure liked to talk about principles whenever it suited him.

xii. My Brother vs. Stepdad/Mom

The night before we were supposed to leave my bag was fully packed with what little I had as a kid. I remember sitting on the couch in my mother's apartment dreaming about the waterfall pools. Suddenly, there was a knock. My older brother was at the door. He told my mother that my father was not going to take us on vacation because of the recent increase in child support. Looking back, this was a very, very child'ish decision that was almost certainly a lie. But like my father, my brother is very impulsive and almost completely void of self-control. I am convinced it was a setup and ploy to pit us against our mother. The sad part is, it kind of worked. Keep in mind I was 11.

My brother yelled, "Where's your boyfriend at?" My stepdad walked into the room with his leopard-spotted underwear on. Trust me when I say that is not an image I ever want to see again. My brother then reported that we would not be leaving for vacation tomorrow given my mother's recent child support increase. He shoved her against the door and yelled at her for about fifteen minutes. I don't remember what he said. I was hiding in the other room and almost wet myself. I was a very nervous, scared kid. I had very good reason to be.

My mother later told me my brother kept looking out the front window of the apartment. Someone was in the vehicle with him. I was later told it was one of his friends. To this day, I wonder if my dad was in the car with him. I cannot prove it, but I believe my brother was "sent" on this mission.

We were very scared my brother would come back after he finally left. While my dad did not own a gun, my brother associated with some very unsavory types who had God knows what. We left and stayed at my stepdad's home for the night.

My father later confessed that he "let it be known" in the community that if he caught my mother's attorney in a dark alley, he would beat him to death with a baseball bat for garnishing his wages and asking for an increase in child support. I can still picture him telling me this as he stood at his kitchen sink. "I'll beat that mother f***er to death with a f***ing baseball bat, don't think I won't." Keep in mind I was 11.

xiii. The Start of Sixth Grade: Granby, Missouri

My stepdad's place was on the wrong side of the road for me to stay in Neosho schools. This was upsetting as what support I had came from some lifelong friends I went to school with and a few high-quality teachers along the way. I had to start at a new school as my mother purchased a singlewide trailer and plopped it on my stepdad's property. As an aside, my grandparents signed for the trailer as my mother's credit was ruined from her first bankruptcy. When she filed her second bankruptcy, creditors repossessed the trailer after my mother moved in with my second stepdad. I was told my mother joked at lunch when confronted about the repossession, "What are they gonna do? Dig up my parents' grave and take the money from them." I can see why creditors behave the way that they do.

I was nervous at the start of that first day. Thankfully, I got in with some nice-enough people. But Granby schools were not good for me. They were years behind where I was at Neosho and did not have the same opportunities for me as a bigger school like Neosho would.

About halfway through the semester, I became depressed. I seriously missed my friends and wanted to return to Neosho. This was the days before social media, cell phones, and text messaging. If I wanted to talk to my friends, it meant long distance charges and so I was almost completely cut off from them. My mother worked for a small feed company in Neosho and commuted to work each day. My stepdad's place was only about ten minutes from Neosho. I created a proposal that was reluctantly accepted. I would use my dad's address and attend Neosho schools.

When I returned, it felt like a reunion. I was very happy. My mother took me to school, and my dad picked me up. He would drop me off at his house where I would stay until my mom picked me up after work. He even had a drawer of candy where he put my favorite Reese's® peanut butter cups in there.

Now granted, the more time I spent in Neosho the farther I grew from my mother. While I've never been told this, I believe my father picked up on this. I think he then used it against me. You see, my father hated paying child support. To this day, he still complains about paying off my mother's credit card bills from her first bankruptcy, my mother's attorney who he frequently referred to as "Perry Mason," and the increase in child support. At the time, he was in substantial debt and needed every penny. He saw an opportunity and capitalized on it. My father started being very nice to me. Bought me all kinds of things, including the candy I liked so much. My mother could not afford this type of treatment as my father made considerably more money than my mother.

xiv. Allergies

It was not until I was 25 years old that I learned I suffered from very severe seasonal allergies. Growing up, I would get sick every time the weather changed. Given that I grew up in southwest Missouri where you could literally experience all four seasons in one day, I was routinely sick. I spent the first quarter of my life untreated from a very treatable illness even though I had health insurance. The problem was my father and mother would not take time off work to take me to the doctor.

One Saturday evening on one of my "dad's weekends," I accompanied him to a friend's home. He hired the wife of a friend of his to clean the apartment he lived in. They invited us over for dinner. Unknown to us, this family had a cat that spent time indoors and outdoors. We had a cat growing up named Smokey and Smokey never bothered my allergies. But Smokey was an outdoor cat and I very rarely petted her. The cat at my father's friend's house was very friendly and I was very bored as I was the only child in attendance. I began playing with the cat and noticed my eye started itching. Well I was the kid who whenever something itched, I scratched. I went to the bathroom and discovered that my eye had swollen shut from all the itching. When my father learned this, he intended to just take me home so my mother could deal with the problem. His friend's wife instructed him that this was inappropriate, and he needed to take me to the hospital. He had been drinking and did not care for this unsolicited parenting tip.

After taking me to the hospital, my father was so annoyed with the whole situation that he took me back to my mother's house. I asked if I could stay with him because I wanted to see him. He made up an excuse I do not recall, but basically said no. I believe he said it would be "easier" to administer the eye drops at my mother's home. I did not understand that response and I still don't.

xv. The Bike

When I turned 12, my mother asked me what I wanted for my birthday. I asked for a new bicycle. Mine was rather old and I was hopeful for a new one. Nothing crazy expensive like a road bike, just something simple or something similar from Wal-Mart. My father issued a check for $35.00 that I gave to my mother to put towards the bike. She told me that this amount was not enough from my father and he needed to give me more.

Now granted, the two of them should have communicated to resolve this issue. But because we are dealing with adults behaving like children so that did not happen.

When I told my father what my mother said, he wrote a new check for $65.00. He then held it up and showed it to me while driving, eyes nowhere remotely close to being on the road. He then shouted, "Ya know what I got when I was a kid?" I shook my head as I had no idea what he was going to say. He held up the check and covered up the six on the 65.

I felt so guilty I no longer wanted the bike.

xvi. How I Told My Mother

It's funny. Even though my father has a horrible temper, and routinely threatened to beat people with baseball bats for minor infractions, he avoided confrontation like the plague. I believe it is because he has some very deep-rooted insecurities and is almost entirely lacking any remote speck of self-confidence. When I told him I wanted to move in with him, he made me tell my mother. Any self-respecting parent would have had an adult talk and figured out their child's living situation. The problem is we are not dealing with adults here. We are dealing with rage addicted, drug addicted, pill addicted people who have very severe, untreated mental health problems. It's essentially a Heinz 57 blend of some really bad shit.

I remember this moment just as vividly as I remember seeing my brother's body go flying off the front porch. We pulled up to my step-dad's house as they were eating outside. I asked to talk to my mother privately. I told her I wanted to move in with my dad. I did not care for my stepdad and his drinking, and my dad was treating me nicely at the time. Her first response that I will never forget: "What am I going to do about child support?" It took me years to process this. Picture a 13-year-old kid telling his mother that he was moving out and the first sentence that pops out of her mouth is a concern about money. What a loving family.

You see, my mother and father were both very money hungry people. My father more so than my mom. My grandfather on my mom's side once commented that my father falsely believed there would be a bank vault behind the Hurst for my dad's funeral. My mother always struggled with money because she had a very serious addiction to antidepressants.

I do not remember how I responded to my mother when she asked me about child support. I later learned in counseling that sometimes our minds will block out certain memories as a defense mechanism because they are too painful to remember. I believe this defense mechanism kicked in at that moment. I walked outside crying and my stepdad asked what happened. My mother responded that I was moving in with my dad, "because he has money." What a day.

xvii. Merry Christmas

While I do not recall which year, I remember my father and I at Wal-Mart one December getting groceries. I was saving my allowance money for weeks to buy him something nice for Christmas. Granted, I did not get much allowance money so "nice" was a flexible adjective in my book. And I was too young to have a job of my own. My father told me he wanted some new sweatpants and a sweatshirt. I bought him two pairs of sweatpants and a new sweatshirt. I was very happy and pleased when I gave him his gift as he said that is what he wanted.

Weeks later, he was in the kitchen talking about Christmas. He was disappointed that he did not get more for Christmas. His words, "Only two pairs of sweatpants and a sweatshirt? Merry Christmas and Happy F***ing New Year." I was very sad, but it was all I could afford.

xviii. My Father, the Magician

I quickly discovered that my father's kindness was extremely temporary with a very obvious hidden agenda. He got me moved in to avoid paying child support and had my mother pay us directly. He was hopeful this monthly stipend would cover all our living expenses. What he failed to realize is that kids are more expensive than he initially thought.

My father first started avoiding me. You see, I was very scared as a kid. I was afraid of almost everything. Bugs, the dark, my own shadow. I later learned this was a major symptom of Post-Traumatic Stress Disorder from all the violence I witnessed as a child. I was also very small for my age, so it made me an easy target for bullying, both at home and abroad.

My father would work until almost midnight every night by choice. I remember sitting on the couch one summer night talking to him on the phone. I begged him to come home. He wouldn't. He didn't want to.

I remember in seventh grade I was nominated by my teachers for a citizenship award called the Daughters of the American Revolution award. I later learned that parents of the award recipients were notified in advance via a letter so they could attend the ceremony. My father got the letter, did not tell me congratulations, and then did not show for the awards ceremony. I remember this is the second time I truly felt alone.

Thankfully, when my name was called, my friend's dad saw me standing there alone and pulled me to stand by him. I never forgot that.

That evening, I confronted my dad about why he was not present for the ceremony. He said the letter had the wrong date on it. I find that discovery fascinating as his was the only correspondence with the wrong date while every other parent of an award recipient had a letter with the correct date on it. My father routinely generated bullshit lies.

xix. A Computer for School

As I moved up in my schooling, it became clear to me that I was intelligent and insecure. While I had some very generous academic gifts (a photographic memory, for one), I was a deeply disturbed person. The worst part is I did not fully realize it until many years later. Instead, I smiled and convinced everyone I was truly happy even though I was completely miserable.

I asked my father for a computer for school. My classes started to require typed reports for various things, and I needed a place to work. Mind you this was not for gaming purposes or anything related to personal entertainment. I asked for a computer for educational purposes.

I remember we went to Subway for dinner that night. My father was saying he was not sure about the computer and that we could go to Springfield (60 + miles away) to "look." I told him I did not understand why I had to go with him if we were just looking. He slammed his fist on the table and yelled, in the middle of a restaurant, "God damn it, you have ridden me like a F***ing bicycle about that mother F***ing computer." Even though he was not finished with his sandwich, he got up from the table and stomped out of the restaurant like a child. As he was walking out, he ranted, "I'll be in the truck waiting."

Humiliated, I took a few more bites from my sandwich and walked out. I later called him to apologize, which I never should have done because it was not necessary for me to apologize for anything. He said, "You'll learn."

xx. Bills & Notes

Having two kids at home for a single parent was no doubt financially difficult for a man without a college degree. Now granted, my father made over $100,000.00 a year because he literally worked every second that he could. But when you are poor at managing money, have a very severe addiction to some disgusting pornography, and give child support directly to your two kids, that $100k runs out pretty quick.

I remember coming home from school one time and there was a note on my television. My father left me notes routinely. They were all bad. I have spent many hours in therapy recalling these notes. I told one therapist my father used me as an emotional punching bag. Here's how. Whenever he had a bad day, rather than attempt to be surrounded by your family and friends, my father would habitually resort to yelling, cussing, and the occasional throwing/breaking of a thing or two. His favorite thing to do to torture me was leave me notes on my tv. These notes were always double spaced, with various words underlined for emphasis, and always filled with hate. One exemplary note told me how bad his day was, how much the bills were that month, how he lost his keys in a parking lot and had to go back to get them in the rain. He then ended the note with, "I hope you're having a good day." He didn't hope that.

One of the biggest struggles I have faced in my life is the commandment to "Honor thy Father and thy Mother." Given who my parents were/are, I have come to the realization that they were not a mother or a father to me and therefore do not deserve to be honored as I have been Biblically instructed to do so.

In high school, I was a superstar. President of my class, Championship A Policy debate team, Key Club President, National Honor Society, 4.0+ GPA, top 10 of my graduating class, name constantly in the paper. You name it, I did it. My father started receiving numerous compliments from locals at The Donut Shop where every person in my hometown seemed to congregate for breakfast. For the record, those are hands down the best doughnuts I've ever had so it makes perfect sense to see record breaking attendance on a daily basis.

One of my father's biggest faults is an extremely delicate ego. He is also a very proud man. These compliments gave him an idea. Privately, he would still treat me like shit because he, to this day, still views me as a mistake. Publicly, however, he could advertise me as a trophy to show off "his success as a parent." If they only knew.

My father started bringing my debate trophies to work to show his coworkers. Given how my father behaved, I'm genuinely surprised none of his coworkers ever harmed him physically. I don't advocate violence, but I know how humans can be.

Aunt Mary later told me that my dad called her one night with an "idea." I have a Great Uncle whose nickname was "Cotton" who lived in Twin Falls, Idaho. He was a multimillionaire who lived in an enormous mansion. I never saw it, but I'm told that there is a waterfall inside the home. When I was younger, my father asked to borrow some money from Uncle Cotton who refused. I think that rejection never left him.

The "idea" my father shared was to send a letter with news clippings attached. The news clippings contained example after example of my success. He wanted the no-doubt loveless letter to close with, "See what we did." I think this was his way at "getting back" at Cotton for not lending him that money years ago. I do not know if this correspondence was ever transmitted. If it was, it no doubt permanently severed a family relationship as I never saw Cotton again and he's dead.

With all this going on, I became very confused. Why would my father show me off in public, then leave me hateful notes and treat me poorly in private? It did not make sense to me…at the time. I later heard a sermon about forgiveness and something the pastor said stuck with me: "hurt people hurt people." My father was hurt very deeply and never sought any counseling or mental health treatment even though he was, at a minimum, a manic bipolar depressant.

xxii. Helping in the Shop

One would think that a father would want to teach his son all the knowledge he possesses. Such was not the case with my father. Here are two quick examples.

The first was on my first car, a 1996 Pontiac Sunfire GT. It was a 5-speed manual transmission. I loved that car. I found a special gear shifting knob at Wal-Mart and wanted to use it to replace the current knob. When I took it to my dad, it of course took him forever to make time to install it. One Sunday, he finally said I could come out to the shop so we could install it. He was having a hard time getting the current knob off. I made an observation in a good-faith effort to assist. His response was to put the tools down and say, "Okay, mechanic, you can fix it." I did. I have never seen him more annoyed.

The second was when I was helping him move something with a forklift. Although I had zero training and barely a drivers' license, I was chosen to operate the forklift. OSHA violation aside, I was trying to be as helpful as I possibly could. I got the forklift stuck in some mud and come to find out forklifts do not perform well when stuck. I alerted my father, and he turned around and started screaming. His exact words, "This is what we call a f*** up." I think the "F" word is his favorite word.

xxiii. No Pop in the Fridge

My father drinks soda pop like it is going out of style. He loves Mountain Dew. Despite all the health warnings, he drinks probably three per day (if not more). One time he came home from the grocery store and was unloading groceries. He wanted a cold soda, so he naturally opened the fridge. The problem is my older brother is extremely lazy. He routinely failed to do chores he was repeatedly told to do due to genuine lack of effort and almost no sense of respect for his elders.

The other problem is my dad is very bright but also an idiot. He had a fridge with an auto ice maker in it. Yet despite this, he used ice trays. To this day, he still uses ice trays. For those who do not know, an ice tray is an ancient, primitive form of technology that is a plastic container that you fill with water and place in the freezer. After the water freezes, you empty the ice in a metal tray and then repeat the process as desired.

With the ice bin empty because my brother was too lazy to fill it, and no cold soda in the fridge for the same reason, out came rage dad. This time, for added effect, he hurled empty soda cans like hand grenades that literally exploded all over the kitchen. I was in the basement at the time, but could very clearly hear what was going on as could the rest of the neighborhood no doubt. I was so scared I ran outside with my heartbeat around 200 thinking I was going to die.

This all occurred because there was no cold soda pop in the fridge.

xxiv. "He Signed Up. He's Going."

My father served in two branches of the military: The Air Force and the Army National Guard. He was extremely passionate about his time in the Air Force. The National Guard, not so much.

My father's stint in the Air Force was not very long. Although an extremely gifted mechanic who can easily fix anything, his temper usually gets the better of him. He got sideways with a Colonel and decided to cuss him out. Shockingly, this type of behavior is a no-no in the military. He lost his stripes, aka, he was demoted. When you're demoted in the military, you make less money. Disgruntled, he then used my grandmother's deteriorating health condition as an excuse to obtain an Honorable Discharge and then came home. There is nothing honorable about what he did.

When the war in Iraq kicked off years later, his National Guard unit was activated. My father very much did not want to go. My aunt offered to move down to Neosho to take care of my brother and me. My father refused.

My father's concerns for not wanting to go to Iraq is he would make less money and would have to pay child support to my mother as my mother would no doubt want us to move in with her. He was very adamant that we would not move in with her.

At the time, I attended a local church where the pastor was a very kind man. My father did not attend church. He thought churches were for hypocrites. Despite his lack of faithful attendance, my father manipulated the pastor into assisting my father in obtaining a reprieve from service. I think to this day that pastor helped my father because of me.

Luckily for my father, there were some facts helpful to his case. My first stepdad had recently been charged for beating my middle stepbrother with a garden hose. He had a lot of issues. My dad used this fact to help bolster his claim that my mother's home was "unfit" and that his children needed a "good parent." Of course, my father did not satisfy that description whatsoever, but he made his case at least presentable.

My aunt Mary, who my father does not care for, also assisted him despite his lack of kindness. She contacted a higher up military official and explained the situation. The military official's response was, and appropriately so, "He signed up. He's going."

Days before deployment, our local state representative contacted my father and reported he received a reprieve. He never went to Iraq to serve his country despite pledging to do so. One member of his unit confronted my father by commenting that my father used his kids to avoid serving his country. That man was correct.

To Summarize, my father used the pastor of a church he did not attend, a sister he did not love, and a child he did not want to avoid service to a country he swore an oath to protect. I know some amazing soldiers. He's not one of them.

To this day, my dad collects a retirement check from the military for twenty years of service. I do not know if this book will change that or not.

xxv. The AM Trip to Joplin

Speech and debate is a very rigorous activity. It requires many hours of practice and work to compete at the highest level. Thankfully, I had a wonderful speech and debate coach at my high school who showed me the value of hard work.

I remember we once competed at the Joplin tournament. Because Joplin was only about a twenty-minute drive, this trip was not considered an overnight trip. We routinely had overnight trips throughout the season, but this was not one of them.

One thing about my father is he loves to sleep in. I do, too. The problem is when I was in high school, I would count on him to help wake me up for these early morning tournaments, so I did not miss anything. My debate coach had a very strict attendance policy, so I did not want to disrespect him.

For this particular tournament, I thought we woke up late. We then rushed hurriedly as my father drove me to Joplin to take me directly to the school where we were competing. When we arrived, I learned that I had the wrong time and we were about an hour early. My father did not speak to me all the way home.

When he pulled in the parking lot of my high school to drop me off, I told him goodbye. He threw his truck in reverse and screamed his tires pulling out of the parking lot like a maniac. All my debate teammates witnessed this. Again, I was humiliated and embarrassed.

Keep in mind this public display of affection occurred because I thought I woke up late.

xxvi. My 17th Birthday

When I turned 17, my father took me to lunch with a promise to take me shopping afterwards. My favorite restaurant growing up was Olive Garden. I really liked their breadsticks and salad. That's where I chose to go to lunch.

On the way to Joplin, there was a person I was trying to pass. I was hungry and when I get hungry, I tend to get "hangry." This person was driving rather slowly, and I have a bit of a heavy foot. I attempted to pass this person and they swerved in front of me. My father, riding in the passenger seat, slammed his hand on the dashboard and said, "God damn it, if you take the sidewall out of this thing, you are still going to have to f***ing drive it."

When we arrived to lunch, we sat in complete silence and he would not look at me. He did not take me shopping afterwards. He asked me to return him home and I did. My brother later called me and said my father threatened to throw me out of the house.

This all occurred because I unsuccessfully tried to pass another person on the highway on my way to lunch for my birthday.

xxvii. A Late Night Snack

After helping my father at work one evening, we ventured to Sonic for a late-night snack. I believe the Sonic in my hometown closed at 10:00 PM at the time. My father always has been a slow driver. I do not understand why. My aunt once told me of a tale when he was younger where he almost flipped his car on a turn. I believe that genuinely terrified him. He was also a racer, so I think normal driving was supposed to calm and slow in his mind.

I was anxious to get to Sonic before they closed for two reasons. One, I was hungry. Two, we did not have any snacks at home. I asked my father to drive a little faster and then when we got to the store, the illuminated sign clicked off. I was frustrated. He was "frustrateder."

He started yelling, screaming, and cussing. He told me how ungrateful and spoiled I was. He was so mad this time that after he dropped me off at home, he peeled out of our driveway and drove off.

Remember that my driveway was gravel and he didn't wait for me to get a safe distance away. His spinning tires threw rocks in every direction. Thankfully, none hit me.

I do not know where he went. I do not recall him returning home.

xxviii. Dinner with a Friend

I attended a church growing up and, thankfully, there were some good individuals who worked with the youth group. One of them was a very wealthy and successful businessperson who lived in a mansion outside of town. I asked if he would have us out to dinner to speak to my dad. I was very concerned for my father spiritually as he did not go to church and did not have a relationship with God.

My friend obliged. He invited us out and his wife prepared an amazing meal. This businessperson spent hours with my dad talking to him about everything. I left the evening with a sense of peace about my dad's spiritual future.

The next day, my father was at his shop with his friends discussing the meal from the night before. He remarked, "I wonder what that rich guy thought when he saw me pull up in my piece-of-shit truck." He laughed. The evening had zero impact on his spiritual future. To him, it was all a joke.

I later apologized to the businessman who was very gracious in his response. He told me he did it for me and not for my father.

xxix. Grand Central Station

Growing up, my father was almost never home. You could count on him to come home for some meals and to sleep. That was about it. My brother and his crew quickly discovered this fact and accordingly made my house their headquarters for all kinds of debauchery. My father used to complain constantly, claiming that my brother turned his house into Grand Central Station. This seemed like a bit of a stretch given we were mainly talking about four or five teenage boys hanging out somewhere after school. Keep in mind my father was not there, so I never really figured out why it bothered him so much.

Nevertheless, my brother had one particular friend who my father did not care for. Aside from a major drug addiction, the guy was actually very nice and pleasant to be around. My father, I think, feared that this drug addiction would have a negative impact on his son. He decided to confront my brother about the situation.

I was in my bedroom pretending to be asleep when this happened. Much like when the fridge was empty from soda pop, my heart rate spiked. I can still remember lying in bed clamping my eyes shut as tight as they could be as I guess I reasoned that would somehow make me safer.

My father started yelling at my brother. Again, I'm not sure why he started the conversation with a yell. But that was his knee-jerk response. I do not remember exactly how it started, but at one point my brother interrupted. My father raised his voice to the top of his lungs and must have heaved his hand up in the air. He yelled, "I'm not f***ing finished yet." I then heard glass shatter.

Our dining room table at my dad's was shaped like an octagon. The exterior was wood, and a middle glass piece provided an area on which to set plates, cups, and the like. Or at least it used to. Afterwards, I walked out of my bedroom to see what happened. There was glass literally all over the place. To this day, I am very surprised that my brother did not get seriously cut from the shatter. I'm also surprised my father did not need stitches.

When I offered to help, he told me no and to go away. I did.

xxx. Treating a Piece of Equipment

Although my father routinely complained that he was the, "N*****
Mechanic" at his place of employment, I do believe he genuinely enjoys fixing things. For reasons unknown, some of his coworkers per his
testimony do not treat the equipment very well that he then has to fix.
He is well known for violent outbursts directed at his coworkers when
they tell him about a repair that is needed. Now mind you that linemen have a tough job. They have to work outside in all the elements
and when the power goes out, they hardly sleep. I remember my father
would routinely complain about their reports to him for repairs. One
report was about no air conditioning and he complained that the linemen wanted to drive a "Lamborghini." He even reportedly called one
coworker a "knuckle-dragging mongoloid" when the linemen made
an honest mistake with his truck. I am genuinely surprised my father
never got the living piss beaten out of him by a coworker.

My father would routinely tell me that, "This is not how you treat
a piece of equipment." I never understood this. Equipment was made
to be damaged as the job they have to do is difficult.

But that equipment was very precious to my father. My father
treated his equipment like his children, and his children like equipment. The sad part is I know his children will most likely not be at his
funeral. I sure hope Truck 22 shows up.

xxxi. Back in with Mom

When I was 17, I had a Chevy Blazer. I was driving through the
parking lot when I accidentally ended up in a ditch. I thought that the
road continued and could not see. It was a stupid mistake, but an honest one. The security guard from our school came over and he helped

tow me out. I was very scared. Come to find out the only damage was a cracked oil pan and a broken bumper, which was very cheap (and easy) to fix. What happened next haunted me for many years.

I arrived home and called my dad to tell him what happened. Now most parents would be genuinely concerned for the safety and well-being of their child involved in an auto accident. This concern could not have been further from my dad's mind. I was crying and my dad asked what was wrong. He said, "You didn't get in a wreck in that new car, did you?" Keep in mind the car wasn't new but instead many years old. I started crying harder. He screamed and started cussing. I do not remember what he said but he eventually slammed the phone down on the receiver.

I went and stayed with a friend that night as I was scared of my father. I had no money. He never called to check on me to see where I was. My friend bought me a doughnut the next morning for breakfast as I did not have any food. Another friend (the son of the man who pulled me to his side at that seventh-grade awards ceremony) bought my lunch as I had no money or food. The friend who bought me the doughnut then took me out to my dad's shop later that afternoon. Keep in mind my father had frequent visitors at the shop because if you wanted to see my dad, he was working all the time.

I walked in and saw my dad working. When he saw me, the expression on his face was pure disgust. He said, "What do you want?" I asked if we could talk. He responded, "Not here, later." I started to exit, but apparently not fast enough in his mind. Then he yelled at me and said, "Go on. Get!" as if I were a dog. I ran to my friend's car crying, ashamed, and embarrassed.

That evening, he came home. I was downstairs in the basement doing homework. He came downstairs to my room and started yelling/cussing (common). He told me he intended to fix the vehicle and sell it. I asked him if I was nothing more to him than a lost paycheck. I do not recall his response. I believe this is once again one of those moments my brain will not let me access because it is too painful for me to remember.

So, I decided to move back in with my stepdad and mom. I remember calling my father to tell him of my decision. I told him I wanted to use his address so I could stay in Neosho schools as it was my senior year of high school. His response, "If your mother takes me back to court for more child support, YOU will be sorry."

I have zero doubt to this day that if my mother had asked for additional support then my father would have contacted the school to let them know I attended there "illegally."

xxxii. The Board of Governors Scholarship

I took the ACT four times in high school. My scores were 25, 25, 27, and 28. This is frankly a miracle as I had horrific, untreated anxiety and PTSD. At 28, Missouri State University would bestow their Board of Governors Scholarship. This covered full tuition. I was elated. Nobody in my family had ever graduated from college, and nobody ever attended a major university like Missouri State. I remember sitting on the couch of my mom's singlewide calling my dad to tell him the wonderful news. His response, "That's great, but you're gonna get more money, right?"

His prophecy turned out true as I did get more money. I got a few scholarships for leadership awards and a debate scholarship. I graduated undergrad with only $3,000.00 in student loan debt from my first year. Never a congratulations or a thank you; only an endless expectation that I should have done more.

xxxiii. Missouri State University

One of the best decisions I ever made in life was to become a Bear. Missouri State was truly a special place that opened immeasurable opportunities for me. Like in high school, I was a star undergraduate. I had a 4.0 GPA, a slew of leadership positions and associated awards, and was even appointed by Governor Roy Blunt as the Student Governor for the Missouri State University System Board of Governors.

It was in undergrad for the first time that I attended counseling. Missouri State had a program where students got 7 free counseling sessions from graduate students studying psychology. I do not remember much about those counseling sessions, but I was becoming aware that I had some very disturbing pain. At Missouri State, I started meeting some people and seeing how children should be treated. Their parents helped them with school expenses considerably as they had planned financially for their children's success. They regularly came to town to visit. They would send care packages, loving notes, and encouragement on a daily basis. I had very little of that.

While I was seeing other kids being treated a certain way, I started to question things. What was wrong with me that I do not receive such treatment? I also wondered what I had done to deserve my childhood. I even asked God these questions and remained horrifically angry at him for many years because of the stories in this book.

Perhaps most importantly, I started noticing there were things "off" about me. I was easily startled, had very inappropriate rage-filled responses to minor life problems, and loved working. I was slowly turning in to the man I despised.

xxxiv. Graduation Day

You can imagine how excited I was on graduation day. I was about to do something that not one person in my entire family had ever done: graduate from a major university. My father claimed to have an associates' degree, but I have never seen it. Nobody ever claimed to nor did they actually possess a Bachelors' degree.

My father and brother met me at my apartment before graduation. We traveled to the ceremony together. After the ceremony, we went to a hibachi restaurant as that was my favorite. The speech and debate coach I worked for in college joined us for lunch. She observed my brother's appearance and commented that she could not believe how much my brother and I look alike. He responded, "Yes, but I will never be as smart as him." He then walked out of the restaurant. I told my boss it had nothing to do with her.

Aunt Mary followed into the parking lot for my brother along with my mother. I did not see, nor could I hear, what was happening. Aunt Mary told me everything later.

Come to find out my brother basically overdosed on meth (his current drug of choice) the night before. He was in the parking lot bawling, calling himself a failure, a druggy, etc. My aunt offered to get him help, but said this would be the last time as my brother has asked for "help" before.

Come to find out all my brother really wanted was attention as he hadn't received any all day. Three days later, he went to a rehab place for about three days. He then came back home. To my knowledge, he is still actively cooking, selling, and using meth. It baffles me that law enforcement has never busted him for all his rampant drug usage as he has been a criminal for most of his life.

xxxv. Law School

Let me tell you something, law school is brutal. Not for good reasons, but silly ones. I did well in law school. I was on the law review, captain of a trial team, and performing well academically. But substantial silliness accompanied law school from the environment at the school I attended. It was not the most pleasant three years of my life.

What was more bothersome than my law school experience was the genuine lack of support from my family.

After I found out about my origin story, I wrote my mother, brother, and father letters. I politely told them to go away and never speak to me again. I changed my phone number. I have not spoken to my brother since. I have spoken to my mother once. I attempted a renewed relationship with my dad. It failed. Miserably.

I remember dropping the letters off in the mail. It was like somebody died. In a way, they all did because I swore to never speak to any of them again.

I resumed counseling and met a man who genuinely helped me. He listened, told me it wasn't my fault, and he reminded me that broken people break other people. He was right.

At the start of the second year of law school, I ran into some financial trouble and needed money. Desperate, I called my dad. He never apologized for anything, but he did offer to help me financially. I accepted his help. To this day, I wish I had not.

xxxvi. Hello Credit Cards

My father mismanaged money most of his life primarily because of his porn addiction. Granted, he is a self-made man. Everything he has, he worked for. And he has no problem sharing that fact with every person he encounters whether they are interested in the story or not.

When I got out of law school, I naturally wanted to purchase a home to start building wealth. I applied for a first-time home buyer's loan and learned my credit score was too low to qualify. This surprised me as I always paid my bills on time. Curious, I contacted the lender and asked for an explanation for why I did not qualify.

The lender told me that my debt-to-income ratio was out of balance. I thought it had something to do with student loan debt from law school. It did not.

Come to find out I had significant credit card debt on cards I did not even own. I later learned my father put my name on his credit cards to try and "spread out" his debt. When I confronted him, he told me he did this so I would have access to them in case something happened to him. I genuinely believe that is a bold-faced lie.

It took me years to build my credit score up to a sufficient point to fix that issue.

Below you will read about a situation in my life beyond my control. It was a conversation with my dad while I was in the parking lot of a Pei Wei that forever ended things between us.

Leading up to that conversation, things were starting to get rocky again. I realized I had lived in Tulsa for ten years and not once had my dad come down to stay the night. The most was an afternoon.

At one point, he came to Tulsa, which is in an entirely different state than where he lives. He traveled to purchase a car. He was about a block up the street from my house. He did not call or let me know he was in town. I did not learn about this trip until three weeks later. He said he was "in a hurry" and that is why he never stopped by. I was upset.

One of my father's many character flaws is he sweeps problems under the rug. He has never apologized to me for anything. He would run hours late routinely and tell me to "be patient." His defense mechanism whenever a problem arose was to avoid speaking to the person for a few days, never apologize, and hope the other person would forget the problem ever happened.

So, I was in a parking lot at Pei Wei contemplating whether to be involved in my daughter's life. You will read more about this in the pages to come, but for now, understand she got here along a similar path as me. I basically said I only wanted to be involved if I could be a positive influence and I had genuine concerns on whether I could be such an influence. He told me, "I do not want you to have any regrets for not spending time with the child."

When my father was sent to a third world country as part of his service in the Army National Guard (separate from the Iraq dodging described above), he asked a friend of my aunt Mary to stay with us. The man's name was Bill. Bill was a good guy. But he could see my brother and I had some problems. When my dad returned, and Bill was relieved from duty, Bill visited my dad at work on a Saturday afternoon. Yes, it was a beautiful Saturday afternoon and my dad was working. Bill told my dad that my brother and I were showing signs of problems and my dad should spend more time with us. My father got mad, started cussing, told Bill he knew nothing about parenting, and told him to, "get the f*** out."

I believe his concern about me having potential regrets had nothing to do with my choice and everything to do with his piss-poor parenting.

So, I wrote my dad a final letter. I told him about how my brother sexually abused me, how I never wanted to speak to him ever again, and told him to take me out of his will. I want nothing from him. I consider that day the day my father died.

xxxviii. The Conclusion: Who My dad Is

You must understand that your mind is a very, very powerful organ. It can literally dictate your entire life by what you choose to think. My father chose to bury his demons and never face them. He chose to complain constantly about everything instead of being grateful. He chose to mistreat his children instead of love them. He chose to hold grudges instead of forgive. He chose to hate his offenders instead of empathize with their struggling.

His choices cost him everything. I do not speak to him. His relationship with me almost cost me my life, both as a kid and later as an adult when I very seriously contemplated suicide. My mother divorced him and that left him even further scarred. They do not speak. My brother lives in his basement and is the physical embodiment of my father's parenting. He is hooked on meth, unemployed routinely, and even has a felony conviction for domestic abuse to polish it off. His house is truly a loveless home.

While he is financially well off, my father is not in any other capacity. I fully expect to one day receive a phone call with a stranger's voice reporting they found my father dead from a heart attack. He is in his 60's and still gets as mad today as he did in his 30's. He is a deeply disturbed human being. If you're a praying person, pray for him. He needs it. Badly.

c. Mom

Mom. Where to start. To understand my mother, you have to understand who she was, who she married, and then who she is now. Growing up, my mother's family was very poor. My grandfather worked a dairy farm and had five kids. My mother fell in the middle. She had very little. I remember her telling me a story about how she once walked across town because someone borrowed her "pencil" for school and she needed it to do her homework. Her childhood was not easy.

My mother has started and stopped going to college several times in her life. She's not a dummy. She's actually quite intelligent. But she has depression. Severe, manic, untreated, depression. For those who deal with depression, you know to have a fighting chance that you must attack it. While I do not know why my mother remains untreated, I have a theory. She has a sister who is a "Christian." I put that title in quotes because her sister once told my mother, "If you were closer to God, you wouldn't be depressed." That is, hands down, the worst thing you could tell someone with a mental illness. It also has the benefit of being completely untrue and completely void of any scripture to support such a statement.

i. Mom & Dad

When my mother was in high school, she met and dated my father. They were allegedly a very sweet couple. My father was a wild child. He partied, smoked, drank. On prom night, instead of taking my mother to the dance, he spent it working in a friend's garage.

When my mother was in college for the first time, she was sexually assaulted. I was not alive at this point. It is my understanding a man exposed himself to her and then tried to shove "it" into her mouth. She was alone in a college parking lot when it happened. I do not believe this person was ever caught or convicted. My uncle then followed my mom to and from school while my dad refused because he "had to work." Whenever my dad didn't want to do something, he "had to work."

My mother's first major mistake in life was marrying my father. It is my understanding that my mother was very much in love with my father when they were wed. However, when my father joined the Air Force, he changed. My brother was alive at this point and the family moved from Neosho, Missouri, to Rantoul, Illinois, just outside Chicago. It was over 10 hours away. While I do not know when my mother's depression fully set in, I believe she was depressed at this time. She started missing her family and told my father she was moving back home. She intended to divorce him, a move she very much should have made.

After my father cussed out the Colonel, he moved back home. But he was a changed man. Now fully addicted to "Snuff," my father was a very disgusting human being. I have no issue with anyone who watches pornography. I don't judge people. But I do have an issue with some-one walking around without a filter all the time and using other people like sex objects instead of human beings. My father was the latter.

ii. The First Sexual Abuse

One of my earliest memories in life is very disturbing to me. It in-volves my mother. I do not know how old I was. I was in the bathroom without any clothes on. So was my mother. She advised me that she cut herself "shaving." She was not referring to her arms or legs. She then showed me where she cut herself as the cut was "down below."

Then, the memory stops. Black.

I am thankful I do not remember what happened next as I am confident it was horrendous. Whenever you are sexually abused as a child, it changes you. It makes you different. Your physical boundaries become bigger, you get anxious very easily, and sex looks a little different to you. It did for me.

iii. Cancel Christmas

One of my very first Christmas memories is very dark. I remember my brother and I asked for one of those remote-controlled cars. Thankfully, Santa heard our request and answered our prayers. My brother and I were delighted to open up brand new remote-controlled cars on Christmas morning.

This was in the early 90's and, at the time, the technology for those batteries was not very good. I remember the batteries took four hours to fully charge and that produces a whopping thirty minutes of power. The battery technology was very limited.

Now, as an adult, I would think that purchasing this type of toy would require a little planning. One would think that an adult would plug in the battery early that morning so excited children could immediately play with their toys.

This did not happen. Instead, my brother and I had to wait four hours for the batteries to charge. You can imagine how difficult this would have been for a five-year-old. We were a bit bummed, and we showed it.

I understand this is very much a first-world problem. But it illustrates a good point. My brother and I no doubt complained. I have no recollection of how much we complained.

That night, I was standing in the hallway with my mother standing in the doorway to my father's bedroom. Yes, you read that correctly. I have no memory of my parents ever sharing a bedroom.

I remember they were discussing my brother's and my attitude regarding the remote-controlled cars and waiting for the batteries to fully charge. They both knew I was standing near them and could hear every word.

My mom remarked, "Next year, we should just cancel Christmas."

From that point on, I never looked forward to the holiday season for fear that it may not come.

iv. My mom, the SuperMom

Aside from these transgressions, my mother was a SuperMom early in my life. She did everything. She worked. She spent time with us. She even coached a soccer team although she was the furthest thing from a soccer player. At one point, she left my dad and we lived in a small trailer just outside town for about a week. My aunt told me later that she called and had a deep discussion with my mother. While I was not present for the conversation, I'm confident as to the contents my aunt shared with me. My aunt apparently told my mother that leaving my father (her brother) was a good choice and even offered to assist my mother financially.

You see, my aunt was forced for health reasons to have a hysterectomy at age 28 and never gave birth to her "own children." She treated me like her son. I'm very thankful for that.

After a week, my mother returned to my father and we moved back home. Now that I understand the cycle of abuse, it makes perfect sense why my mother returned home and why I continually tried to please my father.

Throughout my life, my mother had a very hit-or-miss relationship with me. I do not blame her for this. She was depressed, and untreated. That depression robbed her of many things in life. Namely, a relationship with her youngest son.

v. Just Go to The Game

One tradition my high school does for the football team is the "Soap Scrimmage." The junior varsity and varsity football teams spar against one another while the town watches. The admission price for the exhibition is a bar of soap. The idea is the athletes can use the soap after practices and games without the need to purchase it on their own.

When I was younger, I was very attached to my mother. My brother routinely referred to me as "Mamma's Boy" and looking back he was right. I remember a friend wanted to go to the game and I said I needed to ask permission.

We walked back to my house as it was just around the block. My mother, who visibly appeared extremely annoyed, said, "Just go to the game!"

I left. I remember feeling genuinely unwanted.

Looking back, it's ironic how life can be sometimes. A woman who today would probably do anything for a relationship her son once completely rejected him as a small child.

vi. Two Suicide Attempts

During one Wednesday my sophomore year of undergrad, I received a call from my mother, and she alerted me that she was in town. This was odd as the school I attended was about 60 miles from my hometown. Nevertheless, I met her for dinner. She told me she tried to kill herself. Twice. Apparently, her sister intervened and took her to some sort of clinic. I am not sure of this clinic's whereabouts. It happened at an odd time. My first stepdad recently climbed a ladder at work and, despite clear and obvious warnings to the contrary, he stood on the top ring of the ladder. Shockingly, the ladder gave way and he fell about 20 feet, landing on concrete and breaking his ankle. Apparently, workers' comp was not meeting their financial needs and he refused to get another job since he was still getting a check. My mother believed they were financially doomed, and she saw suicide as the only way out.

Again, this is all due to her untreated, unchecked depression.

vii. "I didn't prepare for this."

On the day I graduated from college, I remember riding in the car with my mother on our way to the hibachi restaurant. I was obviously elated. A decorated graduate from a major university has every right to be very happy.

I remember talking to her about law school. I told her I was excited as I always wanted to be a lawyer. I thanked her for pledging to help me. She then revealed that her once promised financial support is not going to happen as she drained her retirement to start a failed dog breeding business with my first stepdad. In her words, "I didn't prepare for this."

Imagine your own mother telling you on the day you graduated college that she didn't think you would be successful. Disturbing.

viii. Post-Undergrad Shenanigans

After I graduated from undergrad, you might recall the scene described previously where my brother exited the restaurant due to his meth overdose. My mother was in the parking lot with him. Aunt Mary told my mother that she thought my mother should be inside as it was an important day for me. My mother responded, "Ryan is going to have more graduations, but [my brother] needs our help." It never really made sense to me why my parents enabled my brother the way they did. Anytime he cried wolf, they came running. And he cried wolf a lot.

After graduating undergrad, my mother spoke to her third husband and my second/current stepdad about me living with them for the summer. I had an internship that summer and was hoping to save most of my money for law school. My stepdad told her I could move in with them, but he was going to charge me rent. My mother defended this decision. The "rented space" to which they referred was a futon in a utility room without air-conditioning. In Missouri summers, the temperature is routinely above 100 degrees. I would have been miserable. Thankfully, my father let me stay with him one more time.

ix. Nowhere to be Found

My mother pledged to help me financially in law school. As you can see above, she later redacted her offer claiming she was 55 and had nothing saved for her retirement. I believe my current stepdad played a considerable role in this decision.

When I was in law school, my mother only spoke to me twice my entire first semester. Your first semester of law school is hands down the hardest. Everything you're seeing and learning is new. The professors are extraordinarily hard on you for what seems like no reason. And you are stressed to the absolute max all the time. Family support is very much needed in this difficult academic time. My mother was absent. When I confronted her about this, she told me the reason she did not speak to me is that my current stepdad was jealous of how much she cared for me. My current stepdad wanted to drive a wedge between us and she allowed him to do so. I do not blame her for this. That is her depression talking. A lifetime of abuse by three terrible husbands will do that to a person.

Four days before my first (and hardest) law school final, Contracts, I received a call from my cousin. Apparently, my mother and my current stepdad got in a fight. My current stepdad got drunk and started throwing her clothes on the lawn at 2:00 AM. I cannot say this for sure, but I believe he was also burning some of them. Honestly, some of these stories have run together over the years so burning may not have been involved.

I took some time and reflected. My cousin and mother's sister/brother-in-law were within walking distance of my mom's home. I was in another state over 100 miles away preparing for final exams working towards a doctorate degree. I advised my cousin that I was not going to speak with my mother until after finals were over as I needed to focus. He then instructed me on "being a man" as my decision signaled to him that I was unfamiliar with the concept.

I spoke with my mother's sister a few days later and learned that my mother was being "needy." My mother and mother's sister lives in a town of less than 2,000 people without even a stoplight. At the time, my mother's sister worked as a retail salesclerk at the only clothing store in town. She had very little to do. I, on the other hand, was in my first session of finals for law school.

Looking back, it is pathetic how these adults behaved. But you must understand that unchecked and untreated mental health problems will produce human beings who behave like these characters I'm describing. It's a pandemic.

After that debacle, I wrote a letter to my mother telling her I wished her the best in life, but I did not consider her my mother any longer. I went ten years without speaking to her. I was recently forced to encounter her. Here is why.

x.   The Hostage Situation

While I still had a relationship with my dad, I asked him to have my mother send me my speech and debate trophies from high school. I'm not a proud or vain person, but I worked very hard in high school debate and had some of the best memories of my life came from that program. I wanted my trophies to remind me of those fond memories. I asked my father to reach out to my mother and mail me the trophies. I even offered to pay for shipping. My mother asked for an address. I gave one. She then asked for MY address.

As an aside, I have no idea if my father ever did this. Given his general avoidance for confrontation, I suspect he never contacted my mother. I may never know.

I refused to give her my address. You see, I know how she thinks and works. She would have driven down here in the middle of the night one night begging me to have a relationship with her. Depression does that to people.

I thought I was "stuck." Thankfully, one of my best friends suggested we travel back to Missouri one Friday night as a surprise and just get the trophies. I actually had the police on standby in case my second-amendment-friendly stepdad decided to aim one of his many guns our way.

When we got to Granby, we drove by my mother's home. I did not use GPS as I will never forget where they live. We drove by and saw the front door open. I drove up the street and discussed with my friend our plan. I thought we should call the Granby police. He thought that might escalate the situation. I had knots in my stomach thinking about facing them. But I knew if I wanted my trophies back, then I would have to face her. I put the car in drive, and we pulled into the driveway about a minute later.

The encounter was awkward. We pulled in and my mother raced outside saying, "Is that who I think it is?" She had aged considerably since I saw her last. I told her I was only there to acquire my speech and debate trophies; nothing more. Sadly, she asked, "Is that all you want?" I said yes. She only had two trophies with her, but they were the ones I really wanted as they were the trophies I earned when I qualified to nationals.

My stepdad walked outside. I said hello and introduced my friend. After getting the two trophies, my mother said the other trophies were in a box in off-site storage. I told her I would send her an address and a check for the shipping fee. I have yet to send her an address.

When my friend and I were getting in my car to return home, my stepdad said, "It's been 10 years. Seems kinda stupid." I told my friend to get in the car. We left. Quickly.

xi. Conclusion: Who My Mother Is

I never intend to see my mother again. I will not be at her funeral. While I do not blame her for anything her depression caused her to do, I do blame her for not seeking treatment. She has insurance. She has a free will. She could have done many things differently in her life. But like all of us, my mother has demons she refused to face. Her refusal to face those demons has left a slew of divorces, bankruptcies, suicide attempts, failed relationships with children, and a questionable relationship with God.

Honestly, I feel truly sorry for my mother. She is, hands down, the saddest person I have ever met.

D. MY LONE SIBLING: MY BROTHER

If my father is the devil, then my brother is his demon. At one point in my brother's life, he was a devil worshipper. I remember he tried to recruit me to do the same. He even boasted that if I started at my age, I could be "burning bibles with my mind" by the time I was his age. Thankfully, I did not venture down that particular path.

Living at home with my brother convinced me that demonic forces exist in our world. I have witnessed and seen his pain. Like my mother, he has many untreated mental health problems. Combining that with a raging hot temper like his father, and a very severe drug addiction, my brother was a recipe for disaster.

i. Early Childhood

Before I became a successful debater, my brother was king. He got everything he wanted. New shoes, tennis racquets, cars, money. You name it; he got it. I got the hand-me downs. It was abundantly clear to me growing up that my brother was preferred, and I was not. Yet despite this preference, I somehow turned out to be "the good kid" and my brother "the bad boy."

The change in my brother started the night my father beat him for trying to steal those pants from the store at the mall. It changed him. Permanently. I have no problem with parents spanking their children when appropriate. This was too far. My brother had welts on his back for days. I believe he even has a physical scar from the beating. I think even my father knew he went too far. After that, my brother was a different kid. He was anxious, scared, nervous. He was not the same fun-loving brother he used to be.

My brother's world got worse after my parents divorced. My brother was 15 at the time and entering a critical part of his youth. He was forming connections with the wrong crowd and walking down a bad path. His problem with drugs opened with marijuana. Many say now that marijuana is not a gateway drug. I believe that to be true, but not for addicts. Marijuana quickly turned into many other things. Acid, heroin, and now, meth.

ii. More Sexual Abuse

When I was still in elementary school, a friend of mine from up the street came over to my house. My brother, my friend, and I were all hanging out in our basement. I do not remember how it started, but my brother encouraged us to all begin "playing with" one another, if you know what I mean. He even convinced my friend to give him oral sex.

I do not know where the inspiration for this idea came from, but I remember feeling very uncomfortable afterwards.

iii. The Benz

When I was in ninth grade, my brother worked at a restaurant in our hometown. He was making significant money selling drugs and doing well as a server. This was all profit as he lived in my father's basement and did not pay rent. Not satisfied with his car, he obtained a loan as an eighteen-year-old for a brand-new Mercedes-Benz convertible. This was in 2001. The car payment was over $600.00 per month.

Within a month or two, my brother lost all interest in the car. Responsibilities usually did not have long favor with him. Mysteriously, I was at home one night preparing for bed when I thought my brother left. I heard the car reverse out of the driveway. I did not think much of it as my brother frequently left late at night for what I assumed were illegal-drug-related errands.

Later that night, I was awoken by my brother and father who were both panic stricken. The Mercedes had been "stolen." I learned the next day that the car was taken to another town and burned in the middle of a field. This all seemed very suspicious even to an untrained eye. I believe my father had State Farm insurance at the time. Not surprisingly, State Farm hired an attorney to investigate the matter and depose my brother. My father had to spend over $10,000.00 in legal fees defending himself and my brother.

In the end, no person was civilly fined or criminally punished for the incident. My brother was saved by a loophole in the law. As my father was the primary insured on the policy, State Farm had to somehow prove my father was involved in the event. My father is many things, but a thief he is not.

To this day, I have no idea if my brother was involved in this incident or not.

After this whole debacle, my brother seemed to want to get his life together. My father spoke with a recruiter who got my brother in the military. I believe it was the Marines, although I honestly do not remember. My brother departed for basic training. His first stop was Kansas City. The military tested him for drugs, and he tested clean. Apparently, when he arrived at basic training in Michigan, he failed the drug test. He was sent home on a bus along with a Dishonorable Discharge.

When my brother returned home, he confessed what happened. Crying at the dinner table, he told my father he had a gun in his mouth the evening before and was ready to pull the trigger.

To be honest, I always thought that is how my brother would go.

iv. *Not My Brother's Kid*

My brother's lone professional success came from the restaurant industry. He has a very gregarious personality and is usually quite friendly. He enjoys conversing with people and is usually not shy. I always believed he would make a great salesman. In any event, my brother began working at a restaurant in Joplin and met a young lady. He confessed at Christmas that she was expecting a child and soon the child was born. The child was a beautiful girl. She brought substantial joy to my brother's life.

A few months later, we learned that the girl had a one-night stand with another man and the child was not my brother's. I felt so bad for my brother when I heard this news. The only time I have ever seen him truly happy was when he was with that little girl.

v. The Moves

At some point, my brother moved to Arizona. I do not know the reasons for this move. It is my personal belief that he got in a bad way with some worse people and needed to evacuate the area. So, he went to an addiction treatment facility in Arizona. I believe this to be his longest period of sobriety since he started using drugs.

Although he stayed in Arizona for many years, his sobriety was very short. He quickly got back into illegal drugs. One night, he and his girlfriend with whom he lived got into a dispute. I was nowhere near the location when this incident happened. From the court minutes I later read online, my brother was charged with a Felony of Assault & Battery against a female. He was forced to take anger management classes as part of his plea deal.

I later found out that after the fight, the girl ran out of the house to her neighbor. It is my understanding this neighbor is a very large man. The neighbor returned to the house and gave my brother a little payback for his transgressions.

He then moved to Colorado for reasons unknown. He did not stay long. His next destination was Florida. He connected with a long-lost uncle of ours who was a very severe alcoholic and drug addict. He then returned to Joplin.

What's interesting about this trek across the states is my father's reaction to it all. I remember him promising me that if my brother moved back to the area, my father would not let him move in. "I won't let him bankrupt me" he would constantly say. I knew it was a front. When it came to my brother, unless my dad lost his temper, my brother always got his way.

Not surprisingly, my brother ended up at a place back in Joplin. While partying one night, he fell off a three-story balcony and was rushed to the emergency room. My father visited and took him back to where he was staying. When my father laid eyes on the accommodations for my brother, he immediately invited him back home. My brother now returned full circle back to where it all began.

vi. Conclusion: Who My Brother Is

My brother is 37 years young at the time this book was written. He has no post high school education, routinely has no job, no savings, no retirement plan, no wife (although he may have a kid in Arizona that he is not involved with), and no future. He has a very severe addiction to meth and many untreated, unidentified, unchecked mental health conditions with zero support system and no access to proper medical treatment.

I try to avoid using the words always and never. But I believe my brother will always be a drug addict and will never recover from the pain of his life.

Like my mother, my brother was not the culprit. Sure, he made some poor choices. But his primary issue has never been drugs. His primary issue was his untreated mental health issues from years of abuse and neglect.

I fully expect to one day receive a phone call from someone letting me know that my brother killed himself. It is sad to issue such a prophecy, but it's something I've always felt would happen.

E. Jennifer

For Jennifer's sake, I have changed her name. Please understand the person I identify in this book as Jennifer is most certainly **not** named Jennifer in real life. Any relation to a real person named Jennifer is purely coincidence.

What may surprise many of you is that I have a child biologically and I am not involved in her life. This may cause many of you to stop reading and pronounce me a hypocrite. I encourage you to continue. If nothing else, it will satisfy your curiosity to hear what happened and why I am not involved.

I was 25 years old when I met Jennifer. I was introduced to her by a friend in law school. Jennifer has a lot of things going for her in life. She's nice, intelligent, hard-working, and caring. She is a schoolteacher and a mother. She would probably make many men happy and content. Not me.

When Jennifer and I met, I never thought it would be long term. We did not go out on dates, if you know where I'm going. I asked Jennifer if she was on birth control. She told me no.

She once drove to my apartment in the middle of a snowstorm so we could be together. When she arrived, I explained that I was nervous about intimacy as she was not on any form of birth control. She then told me three things I will never forget:

1. My ex and I tried to get pregnant for years and it never happened.
2. Doctors told me my whole life that I would have a difficult time conceiving.
3. If I get pregnant, you do not have to be involved.

Not surprisingly, Jennifer soon called me frantic to let me know that she was pregnant. When I reminded her of our conversation and the three promises identified above, she became defensive. Advising that I should be "more of a man" and get involved with her.

Ladies, a quick note. Misleading a man into having a child is one of the gravest offenses you can commit. First, it is fraud in the inducement. If that were a contract dispute, you would be on the hook for punitive damages. Second, you are punishing a man with child support, arrearages, an income assignment, and a load of other financial responsibilities the father never agreed to. Finally, and most importantly, you are harming your child. There is a good chance that the father will not be involved, or, worse, be an ass like my dad.

Consider alternatives, like open adoption. One of my friends from high school did an open adoption and everyone is happy. The children have multiple parents, the biological parents get to be involved, and the adopted parents get to be the primary caregivers for the child. It is a win-win situation for everyone.

Mine is not. I begged Jennifer to do an open adoption. Years later, she told me, "I considered it." If there was any consideration given, it was very minimal.

When I got my first ever paycheck as a lawyer, something I had worked my whole life to obtain, there was an income assignment for child support and past-owed support. I made more money as an intern than I did as a lawyer. I felt like a fool and a failure. I had to move out of the apartment I loved into an apartment complex where gunshots riddled the night and the local police department's gang unit routinely patrolled. I was in a very, very dark place.

Thankfully, things in my career started to gain speed. I was doing well as a lawyer and my paycheck started to reflect it. I got a substantial pay raise when I switched firms, triggering child support services to "reassess" my "responsibilities." That new "responsibility" is $1,309.62 per month for one child.

When Jennifer got her increase in child support, she took our daughter and her mother to Mexico that summer. They bought a nice house out in the suburbs with multiple community pools and the primary entrance to the property is surrounded by large, artificial bodies of water with fountains in the middle.

Now granted, I'm happy that my child has a nice place to live and grow. But still, it is a lot to deal with when you consider how it all went down.

In late 2018, I rededicated my life to Christ. This started my healing process. I thought God was leading me to be involved in Jennifer and our daughter's life. I was wrong. Very wrong.

Although I made a good-faith effort, it was abundantly clear that I did not "fit" in their lives. Jennifer and I could not get along on just about everything. After one fight, her friend called me on Jennifer's phone and called me a "Mother F***er." Admittedly child'ish, but her friend observed that we were having some serious problems.

I did not trust Jennifer for what she did, and honestly resented her for what I classified as "stealing money." What's worst, I started viewing time with our daughter as a burden. I think the want to be a parent is something you either have or you don't. I do not have it. I have never had it. And I do not believe I ever will have it.

So, I wrote the most loving note I could to our daughter, the most honest note I could to Jennifer, and I walked away.

I think Jennifer did love me and wanted to keep me, so she tried to use our daughter to do it. When that didn't work, she then used our daughter as a siphon to obtain monthly support checks. That worked. Sort of. But it came at a much, much higher price. The price is that our daughter will never know her dad while she is a child because despite all the effort I could muster, I could not be a positive influence in her life.

Thankfully, the pain of my absence has been tempered by God. He sent two amazing people into their lives, a married couple whose children are grown. They spend time with our daughter frequently. The husband of this couple is a better dad than I could ever be because he truly loves them. I pray for them daily.

What perhaps may touch most of you is this revelation. When I decided to start my own law firm, I had very little money and substantial bills. But I felt like I was being led by God to do it. I called child support services and filed a motion to modify the child support amount as my new annual income was zero. I remember I got the paperwork filed and just needed to serve it. As I'm writing this paragraph, that paperwork is on my desk even though I have been on my own for over a month. I thought seriously about serving it on Jennifer and watching as the terror sets in that the money she got used to would now be reduced by over $1,000.00 a month.

I do not have the heart in me to do that to someone. I even told the business growth consultant I hired to start my law firm about it. I remember saying, "I will find a way." And find a way I did.

In the event my law firm does well, I intend to assist her more. Some of you may find this concept ridiculous as you struggle to get your ex to pay anything at all. But as a person who has been involved with Child Support Services for most of his life, and a person with a dear friend who is a child support enforcement officer, I can tell you two things. First, the employees at Child Support Services have a very, very, very hard job. I feel genuinely sorry for them as they must deal with a substantial amount of BS and make very little money. Second, I know that for every dollar I give to Jennifer, it will go to our daughter to improve their lives. And that is what matters most.

III.

PART TWO: THE SOLUTION

IF YOU'RE STILL reading this, you may wonder how I haven't exploded. I sometimes ask myself the same thing. It's true, I've been through it. Frankly, I've been through hell. And back. Many times. But the good news I write this to you not as the angry, bitter man I once was. Now, I am an optimist who is genuinely excited about his future. I was able to achieve this state of mind through a combination of techniques I am going to identify below.

I want you to immediately dispel any notion that this process will be easy. It will be hard. Forgiving the four people identified above has been the hardest thing I have ever done. It took 10 years, and I believe I will have to choose to forgive them daily for the remainder of my days.

I do not want you to think I am a complainer. Quite the opposite, really. I am happy I went through the things I went through. Not because it made me who I am today. It did not. But I have figured out that if I can handle what I've been through, I can probably handle just about anything. And the suffering I've been through has allowed me to empathize and connect with others on what feels like a celestial level.

I also genuinely believed God allowed all of this to happen so I could one day write this book in hopes of helping all who read it.

As a disclaimer, I want to share this. I read numerous self-help books on my journey to healing. I watched countless sermons, listened to motivational speakers, went to counseling, took medication (prescription and over the counter), meditated, tried apps, and much more. Everything in its own way helped me with something, even if it was a minor issue. The steps I'm identifying below are what helped me the most. Put similarly, I saw the biggest improvements after completing these tasks.

These suggestions may not work for you. Your pain may be greater than what these steps can heal. If that is you, do not give up! If I had given up, I never would have achieved the tranquility I experience today.

Finally, although these steps are numbered, you do not have to follow them in sequential order. What you are going through is deeply personal. Handle this problem as you see best. Surround yourself with positive influences and have substantial support during this process.

I want to say as a final disclaimer that I do not have a relationship with any of the individuals described above. Nor do I intend to. The toxicity of my biological family is horrific. I had to forgive them from a distance. I do not love them, but I no longer wish them harm or ill will. I just want all our remaining days to proceed as they should: in peace.

The only caveat to the paragraph above is I intend to have a conversation with my daughter when she is old enough to understand what is going on. I intend to do two things. First, I am going to explain to her what happened by telling her the origin story described above. I may even give her this book. Who knows? Second, I will apologize.

So, here's the solution: forgiveness. It's the only way. It's a simple concept, yet it's extraordinarily difficult to accomplish for many of us. It becomes especially difficult when the offender has never apologized and thinks that he/she has done nothing wrong. Don't worry, you can still forgive.

Before we get started with the steps, I want to share that I believed after I got saved that I had found peace. I was wrong. I grew up watching Dragonball Z°. I still watch it to this day, even though I am in my thirties. For those who do not know, Dragonball Z° is an anime series about a group of warriors who protect Earth. The main character is a person named Goku. Goku is part of a warrior race known as Saiyans and hails from the planet Vegeta. In the series growing up, Goku attempted (and failed) on numerous occasions to turn into what's called a "Super Saiyan." This ascended fighter basically doubled in strength and speed. It was not until Goku faced the conqueror Frieza that he was able to finally unlock this form. In the scene where he transforms, lightning shoots through the sky and Goku's hair changes from black to blonde. He is further accompanied by a new yellow aura to confirm his transformation.

Before Goku unlocks this form, he was once engaged in a conflict where he believed he had achieved this new form. He later learned he was wrong. This form was later dubbed the "False Super Saiyan Form." After I got saved, I met my daughter for dinner and decided to get involved with she and Jennifer. I took Jennifer on a few dates as we tried to resolve our issues. But I had nowhere near forgiven Jennifer for what she had done. And not even come close to forgiving my family for their abuse. I was a False Super Saiyan.

My career also made some changes as I left a job I hated and went to a different law firm. It was good for a while. But I knew it was not my destination. I then went to a law firm and things got bad in a hurry. I took a substantial cut in pay and accumulated considerable debt. I thought this was the end of the road for me and my drinking increased significantly. I then started having suicidal thoughts. I located a clinic in a foreign country where physician-assisted suicide is legal and made plans to obtain a passport, present to the clinic, and end my own life.

My realization that I was truly broken came the night I wrote and sent the letters to our daughter and Jennifer. I realized I carried all this around forever and never let it out.

With what felt like a failed career as a lawyer and failure as a father, I hit rock bottom.

I got drunk one night and posted something very controversial on my Facebook page. I apologized the next day. But thankfully some people from my hometown saw it and intervened. They sent me messages and one of them even met me halfway between Tulsa and my hometown for dinner. I think their prayers and attention, and the brief stint I did in A.A., are the things that truly saved me from ending it all.

I knew I needed to dig myself out. I just did not know how. I started attending Life.Church and they were doing a series called, "The Grudge." It was four sermons about forgiveness. After hearing these sermons, and reflecting on all the self-help stuff from my past, I put together this plan.

A. STEP ONE: THE RIGHT MINDSET

Before you can hope to succeed, you must start with a want. Have you ever been around a diesel fire before? This is a bit of my country roots coming out. But for those of you who haven't been around one before, diesel fires burn hot. Very, very hot. They are so hot that you cannot usually have your face pointed towards the fire. Numerous times as a child, I would have to move logs on a diesel fire, and I can remember the sting when your face or another body part got too close.

Your demons are like a diesel fire. They will be hot. They will be tough to face. But you have to face them. Most importantly, you have to want to face them. You cannot hope to succeed if you do not want to face your demons and have a genuine desire to forgive.

B. STEP TWO: IDENTIFY YOUR OFFENDERS & THEIR OFFENSES

This is the hard part. You must start by identifying who it was that deeply hurt you. I do not mean the person who cut you off in traffic or the guy who cut in front of you in line at the movies. I mean bad guys. The rapists, abusers, pedophiles, murderers, and the sort. I was once sitting in an A.A. meeting when a man described a story about a woman who forgave five men who gang raped her. This story led this man to forgive the man who murdered his son. That's who we are talking about.

Do not let anyone dissuade you by saying things like "well, he didn't mean it" or "you should just get over it." Remember, hurt people hurt people. Those individuals are hurting also. They probably just don't know it yet.

When identifying offenses, you may run into what I call "black spots." I shared above where I would have vivid memories that would suddenly end without explanation. In counseling, I learned that our subconscious will sometimes block our conscience mind from reengaging in those memories. Through the years, I've had various individuals present the idea of hypnosis where a therapist will guide me through these memories. I declined to do so. My rationale was my mind blocked those memories for a reason and that's where they should stay in my opinion. You may disagree and want to engage in such a practice. If so, great! I wish you all the best in your recovery.

You may also have certain recollections trigger some very intense emotions. Be prepared for this. For me, it was anger. I became very angry and had to "walk it off." I live right across the street from a park and would frequently walk over there and then come back.

When I was identifying offenses, a flood of them fell out of me for about an hour. Then a few trickled in over the weeks to come. I kept a piece of paper with me and wrote them down. When I stopped thinking of them, I moved on to step three.

You may later think of more offenses. Don't think, "oh no, I have to go back!" Simply jot them down and continue with your recovery.

You may be tempted to type these offenders and offenses given today's digital age. There is a cathartic feeling that accompanies handwriting. Let your computer charge and break out the pen and paper.

Trust me, you will feel better.

As you're doing this, do not judge yourself. Do not think, "well that wasn't really that bad" or "this is something I can just get over." You're carrying it with you for a reason and you're thinking about it for a reason. Get it out.

Finally, do not put any pressure on yourself to finish. This may take a day; it may take a month. Forgiveness is a process, not a switch. Allow the process to work itself.

c. Step Three: Unleash

I have played tennis since I was twelve. A very kind man at the church I attended growing up gave me weekly lessons for $3.00. This man was an older man who had a more traditional playing style. We spent probably double the amount of time on my backhand as we did on my forehand. His rationale (which was a good one) was that most players have weak backhands. So, if you develop a strong backhand, it makes you stand out as a player. And I now have a very good backhand.

When I returned to tennis after college and law school, I realized I really did not know how to hit a forehand. Pro after pro worked with me until one Saturday afternoon when I got the best forehand tip I've ever received. A friend of mine was wrapping up a private lesson with a pro so we could play some singles. I was picking up balls so she could get more time with the teaching pro. The pro saw what I was doing and invited me to join the lesson. This was the first time we met on the tennis court, so he had never seen me play. He hit me a few balls then made an observation about my forehand. In his estimation, my forehand was stronger than my backhand if I made a minor change. His exact words: "let it go."

I'll admit I was nervous to try as my forehand has always been a weakness. But I did what he told me to do. I stepped in, rotated my core, and just swung. What happened next was a complete shock. I just produced the hardest, fastest, "spiniest" forehand of my career.

He said, "Again." And ball after ball effortlessly flew over the net in the same fashion. Now, my forehand is a weapon.

You have to dig deep and pour out every raw, ugly, disgusting human emotion you feel about those who hurt you. Do not judge; just get it out.

This is the part where you crack that huge forehand for the first time. No hiding. No holding back. Take off the gloves. Unscrew the lid. Unleash.

i. Physical Confrontation?

Thankfully, the easiest step follows the hardest one! Once you have identified everyone who wronged you and the wrongs they committed, you have to unleash all your feelings. You can do this a number of ways. Each person and circumstance is different.

You could confront the offender if they are still around. For years, I dreamed of telling my dad off. Every four-letter word I could think of used to rise through my voice as my blood pressure skyrocketed. But I have never confronted my father in person for several reasons. Number one, it wouldn't do any good. I know people who still live in my hometown and see him routinely. He hasn't changed. And I know that he won't. In my father's eyes, he was a great parent. Second, my father is a very violent, little man. If I made him mad enough, I know he would try to harm me. Third, I did not need to confront him in person. I forgave him through this process.

If you decide that a face-to-face confrontation is the way to go, I recommend a few things. First, if violence is a concern, bring someone with you to keep the peace. Maybe even notify your local police department so a standby officer can be present with you. Second, leave any weapons at home. As a lawyer, I can tell you that numerous criminal cases begin with the best intentions. Finally, if it gets heated, walk away. The last thing you want is an assault and battery charge.

For me, I had a unique approach to the physical confrontation.

See, I was very mad as an adult. I used several different outlets to tackle this. The first was running. I ran two marathons and two halves. But I was a very insecure, stick skinny, 5'7" male. So, I turned to CrossFit® and 30 pounds of muscle later (admittedly some table), I am a bulkier, much more confident person.

When I finished my building phase, I considered confronting them. But I am also trained in Tae-Kwon Do. More importantly, I'm a lawyer. Most importantly, violence solves nothing.

So physical confrontation is up to you. Just be careful.

ii. A Phone Call?

Another possible option is a phone call. I contemplated this option as I could say what I wanted to say and see what response I got, if anything. This avoids some of the concerns about a physical confrontation while still allowing for a conversation and possible reconciliation.

Personally, this was not an option for me. I know that my father and brother have horrible tempers and it would only result in shouting. My mother is a manipulator and I know that would not be a productive conversation. I cannot talk to Jennifer as it usually turns into a fight, her getting upset, and me feeling bad.

I recommend using this option if you want to reconcile with your offender. Maybe an old friend who betrayed your trust, or an ex. If this person has a propensity to harm you, then I do not recommend this option. If the person constantly interrupts you, do not proceed with this option. Also keep in mind that this person may hurt you even more if you speak to him/her as this person could say more things to hurt you.

iii. A Letter

I suspect many of you will choose this option. It is what I went with ultimately. As "examples," I am enclosing at the end of this book the letters I wrote to my father and Jennifer. A letter is a strong option for many reasons. First, you can say whatever you want to say without interruption or judgment. Second, it avoids any possible concern of violence from a confrontation. Finally, you can revise any drafts you make.

One dilemma you will face is whether to send the letter. This is an extremely personal choice and there is no right or wrong answer. For me, I chose not to send the letters. I knew my family would not care. If they did, I have blocked all their phone numbers/social media accounts and only my father knows where I live. They would not be able to reach me. I also did not want to reconcile with them, so I did not send them.

Regarding Jennifer, I contemplated seriously on whether to send the letter. Ultimately, I kept it. I may give it to her after our daughter is grown and gone. But for now, I am not going to send it to avoid any additional pain. That's the last thing she needs.

As you can see in both of my letters, I closed with a positive note. I recommend this. Remember, hurt people hurt people. The offenders who hurt you have been through their own life problems and did not deal with it properly. If you are doing this, you are following the proper steps to deal with your pain. Do not put more pain out there. Be the better person.

d. Step Four: Pray/Meditate

i. A Nod to the Agnostic/Atheist

Some of you reading this may either not believe in a higher power or need more evidence to determine whether a higher power exists. I completely respect whatever your faith, or absence thereof, might be. If this sounds like you, I recommend meditation on the letters. Engage in some breathing exercises and read the letters again. If it was a phone call, think about the exchange and remind yourself that you are doing this for you. Nobody else.

ii. To the Christians

This was me. I have been a Christian my whole life, although I have only recently formed a healthy relationship with God. Pray for your offenders. This will be hard to do. You are taking time from your day to use your energy and relationship with God to pray for people who not only hurt you but did not ask for forgiveness. It is hard, but you can do it. If nothing else, just pray, "God, please be with _____. He/She hurt me, and I know they are hurting too. Please help them find peace. Amen"

You can see in my letters I had a very specific prayer for my dad and Jennifer. Those prayers were tailored and written after I had written the first portion of the letters. I will tell you that some very powerful spiritual healing occurred when I wrote those prayers. Even more powerful healing when I said them out loud. The most healing occurred when I meant them.

iii. Other Faiths

I am in no way attempting to offend anyone by saying "other faiths." I just mean if you follow another particular faith, consult your spiritual leader(s) to see what process they recommend. Maybe you pray, maybe you don't? See what resources your spiritual leaders have to offer.

E. STEP FIVE: FORGIVE IN AN ORDER THAT WORKS FOR YOU

This will be different for everyone. Again, it is deeply personal and should only be done in a method that is perfect for you. There is no right or wrong way to do this.

In some of the advice I received, I heard what I call, "The Sales Approach." Some of my friends are very successful salespersons. They tell me when they are training someone new, they try to give them a few quick, easy sales. The idea is to boost their confidence so they can start working on tougher sales. This approach is to forgive the smaller offenders and offenses first. Maybe the teacher who gave you the bad grade, or the church leader who did not treat you the way you deserved. I am not trying to downplay anyone's experiences. Your "order of offenders" is deeply personal and only you can decide who is a grave offender and who is a minor offender. The idea here is to boost your confidence so you can tackle your bigger offenders with ease.

The second approach I call the "Boss approach." I grew up playing video games. I knew that the levels I played usually would not be that challenging because I tended to excel at most video games. What challenged me most were the fights against the bosses. I knew that I had to save all my energy, weapons, and power ups for those fights because that is when and where it mattered. This approach is where you forgive your gravest offender first. For me, I had to forgive my father first. I knew that the tentacles of his behavior were littered throughout my pain and the only way I had a fighting chance was to forgive him first. I also knew that if I forgave him, then I could forgive anybody.

Thankfully, over time, I was finally able to forgive my father. I realized that he is a very disturbed person who buried all his accumulated demons for over six decades. Once I forgave him, I actually now feel sorry for him. I would never wish my father or my father's life on even my worst enemy.

Once I forgave my father, my next gravest offender was Jennifer. But after my father, Jennifer was easy. I just knew she wanted children, was aging when we met, and, taking her statements above as true (although I still wonder to this day how true they are), she probably thought this was her only shot to have a child of her own. While I do not agree with her decision, I understand it.

With my two gravest offenders forgiven, my brother and mother were a piece of cake. They were essentially versions of me. My brother had a similar childhood I did, but never got any help for his addiction issues. My mother just made some bad choices in men that accumulated over time. And she has untreated, manic depression.

The final approach is to just "let it happen." Maybe you do not have an order of offenders or offenses. That's great! In this approach, you simply work the steps and let nature take its course. Maybe you forgive specific offenses, but not the offender altogether. Or vice versa.

The point to all this is personal. Do whatever works for you. Maybe it is a combination of the above. It does not matter because the end goal is the same.

F. STEP SIX: HELP OTHERS HEAL

Numerous psychologists recommend that if you are about to have a nervous breakdown, go do something for someone else. There is very strong healing power in helping another person who is hurt. Maybe there is someone at your school being bullied because he/she is a different race? Maybe someone you love is in an abusive relationship? Maybe your partner did not obtain that big promotion he wanted? Whatever the case may be, seek out those who hurt and let them know they are not alone. And if they choose to confide in you, listen. Don't just nod and say "uhh-huh." Truly listen to what they have to say.

For me, this book was my step five. I have always been told by close friends and various pastors that the world needed to hear what happened to me. To be honest, I was terrified of exposing who I was to the world. Now, I wish I had done this years ago! Maybe for you it's to issue an online post of what you did? Or maybe you submit the letters to a local mental health organization? Or maybe you write volume two of this book? You decide.

IV.

———∽∽———

PART THREE: PEACE

I WAS HOPING that my arrival at forgiveness would parallel Goku's transformation when he became a Super Saiyan the first time. It didn't. I was hoping I would have some blinding light from the sky sail over my body with an announcement from God that, "I am healed." I even looked in the mirror to see if my hair changed colors like his.

It was nothing of the sort. Let me tell you how I knew I had achieved forgiveness. My peace was confirmed seven ways.

The first confirmation was I stopped being angry all the time. Man, was I mad. At everyone. For everything. I have shattered a small fortune of tennis racquets for no good reason. I have broken small household items. I have screamed at drivers in traffic for simply not accelerating fast enough. I have pictured my father's face on the ground while doing a CrossFit® exercise called "slam balls." "Slam balls" involve taking a weighted ball of sand and essentially throwing it on the ground, catching it while it bounces, and repeating this process until your lungs feel like they may explode. Then, one day, I woke up and was no longer angry. The little things that used to set me off on a rage-filled tantrum became fleeting annoyances and nothing more. I still get mad and will probably always have a temper. But my temper is temporary (no pun intended); it is no longer a constant state of existence.

My second confirmation is I stopped fantasizing about physically harming my offenders and wishing bad things would happen to them. I realized that my gravest offender in my life was my dad. I knew that I would not be able to forgive anyone until I forgave him. I used to fantasize about returning to his shop with a baseball bat and a 12 gauge. I dreamed of swinging the bat until I couldn't swing anymore. I would scream, yell, cuss, and make him feel the way he made me feel. I could feel the anger swell up in me like boiling water. I also fantasized about confronting my brother about the sexual abuse. Finally, I used to pray that Jennifer's brakes would go out while she was driving down the highway. Then one day, it all stopped. I no longer dreamed of harming anyone. Instead, I now pray for their protection and blessings in whatever remains of their life.

My third confirmation is I substantially reduced the amount of alcohol I consume. I mentioned above that I did a brief stint in A.A. A.A. is a great program and I truly believe anyone can benefit from their teachings. Mind you I never completed the twelve steps although I believe their twelve-step program has helped many find their peace in life. Even though I introduced myself in discussions as, "My name is Ryan and I am an alcoholic," I knew deep down that I wasn't. What I shared with my fellow members of A.A. was a jagged path overwhelmed with suffering and despair. I did use alcohol as a temporary means of numbing the pain I was experiencing. Then, one day, I just stopped drinking as much. I still go to bars. I still drink. But nothing like what I used to. I just find that I no longer have a desire to live that lifestyle anymore.

My fourth confirmation is I stopped having vivid nightmares. I shared above that I have an eidetic (aka, photographic) memory. I'm not really sure how to describe it, but my brain takes pictures of things. Admittedly, it's a little odd. But it has always been one of my gifts and has helped me substantially in life. It is one of the reasons I believe I excelled in school as I could easily retain vast quantities of information that usually baffled others. Not surprisingly, this gift is a double-edged sword. I would routinely wake in the middle of the night sweating profusely with my heart racing from recalling one of the many horrific life events described above. This is why I believe I drank as much as I did as I rarely had bad dreams when drinking. I believe the answer to be medical in nature as science has proven that alcohol accelerates your ability to fall asleep while precluding access to the deeper, dreamier stages of sleep. It got so bad that I actually used to fear going to sleep. Then one day, the bad dreams stopped. While I have always struggled with sleeping, and still have a tough time falling asleep (I'm a high-energy guy), I no longer fear going to sleep.

My fifth confirmation came from the feeling of freedom that accompanied producing this work. After I wrote the initial draft, I found myself feeling very sad and blue. This is not altogether surprising given that I basically assembled a compilation of the worst experiences in my life and described them in the best detail I could. I telephoned a life-long friend and explained how I felt. She sincerely inquired if I wanted the world to see this raw and real side of myself. I remember pausing as I had not considered that the world would now know everything I had been through. You see, most people did not know I had a daughter. And nobody knew all the horrors of my childhood. But I remember the gut feeling I began to experience once I got all this bad stuff out from inside. I felt free. This freedom I now experience is a feeling I pray all of you find long before thirty-two years of age. While I used to complain about what I lacked in a family, I am now thankful for the many blessings I have in my life. I responded to my friend's interrogatory and explained that the freedom I now experience is something I genuinely love. And I have no problem with the world seeing me for who I really am.

Sixth, I stopped taking my anti-anxiety medications. I used to take prescription strength meds and was on a constant quest for any herb and over-the-counter stress relief I could get my hands on. My current healthcare provider is one of my best friends. I shared the book with her and her husband. I told my healthcare provider how amazing I felt after getting all of the garbage out. I asked if she thought I could stop taking my anti-anxiety medication as I felt I no longer needed it. Her response was amazing. She told me that I was on a low dose anyway so there was no need to taper off. She then congratulated me on my improvement. As of the day of her response, I have not taken a single anti-anxiety medication, prescription or otherwise. And I never looked back.

Seventh, I was tested. And I passed! Here is what happened. I am a bit of a tennis addict. I play all the time with anybody who has a racquet in his/her hand. One of my friends knows this and invited me on Martin Luther King Day to a drill (which is kind of like a practice for fun) from 6:00-7:30. I usually teach Monday nights, but because of MLK Day, the college where I teach was closed. I happily accepted the invitation and drove to my home court: LaFortune Park Tennis Center. At about 5:50, I realized that my friend was not there. This concerned me so I called her. She answered and I asked if she was on her way. She said yes. I then asked if the drill was at LaFortune. She told me no and that in fact it was at a club all the way across town. She then looked at her message and realized that she forgot to list the club and I just assumed it was our home courts. She then apologized.

This may not seem like a big deal to many, and honestly it isn't. But you have who to understand who I was then versus who I am today. The old me would have gone completely berserk. I would have immediately lost my temper, accused my friend of incompetency, started cussing, started throwing things, driven like a maniac to the club and cussed out every person who got in my way, been rude to my friend who forgot to tell me the location of the drill, not enjoyed myself in the slightest, and then felt horribly guilty afterward. Remind you of anyone else described in this book?

But I'm different now. Admittedly, I was a bit bummed. I knew that I would likely miss the first 10 minutes of the drill. I told my friend that it's fine and we all make mistakes. I then drove across town to the drill peacefully. I didn't speed. I didn't cut anybody off in traffic or cuss anyone out. On the way there, I thought about how I was acting and honestly I was amazed at myself. I could not believe how peaceful my behavior was compared to the old me. And when I got to the drill I noticed something. Every single light I hit on the way was either green or very quickly changed to green. When I arrived in the parking lot of the facility, which had a very vast parking lot as it was on a college campus, someone backed out from a front row parking spot. That has never happened to me before until that day. I believe that was God's blessing for me passing the test. I raced inside, quickly visited the men's room, and got on the court. I only missed the first ten minutes and because there was only nine people (there's usually 30), everyone was still warming up. I got to play all the tennis I wanted. My friend and I joked about her not telling me the correct location and had an amazing time playing together. The pros in charge even let us stay after and play, which almost never happens on indoor courts as there are not that many in Tulsa and everyone wants to play.

I believe the Lord confirmed to me that night the conclusion of 32 years of substantial garbage: I am healed.

Please understand I do not love my dad, brother, mom, or Jennifer. But I no longer hate them. For many of you, this may be the goal. Your goal is not to love them, but just to not hate them. That's a perfectly fine goal!

For some of you, the goal may be to love the person again. That's fine, too! If the offenses are grave and numerous, commence the reconciliation with an open dialogue, but be guarded. If this person is still hurting, they may hurt you again. Be mindful of what it was that caused harm in the first place to avoid it in the future.

I am not saying there will not be any lingering effects after you forgive. I have anxiety and PTSD from my experiences. I still have anxiety and PTSD. I believe I will always have anxiety and PTSD. The difference is that I no longer have this lingering cloud of anger inside me, I no longer flip out when unexpected noises occur, and I am just not as "triggered" as I used to be.

Understand that you will always have triggers. If I am ever in a park and I see parents loving their kids, I think back to all my times alone. I just have to accept that my life was that way. I always let the thought come and go. I do not sit there and give it any more energy than it deserves. Once it is gone, I move on.

I hope this process works for you. I hope you can forgive all your enemies and live your remaining days in peace. I hope. Remember, if it does not work, keep going! I am confident there is a process out there for you. I tried several before I finally pieced together a process that worked for me.

I'm confident that if my family could respond to this work, they would say something like this. My mother would tell how she helped me my senior year of college by giving me $75.00 each week. My father would talk about how he gave me his American Express card in college, and I abused it in his eyes. He would talk about all the cars he bought. He would talk about how he paid my rent in law school. My brother would probably echo how much my parents spent on my schooling. All these statements are true, my parents did give me money over the years. What I would say is any support they gave me came with a much higher price than I should have had to pay, given the abuse detailed above. Regardless of who is "right," they are all forgiven to me.

Some of you may read this and seek out the individuals identified in this book. With the internet, privacy is a thing of the past. You could probably easily identify these individuals and contact them. You may be tempted to give them a piece of your mind. Some of you in my hometown may feel the need to confront these individuals. You may even wish to contact me with something negative. But if you do that and say something harmful, you will only be adding another layer of pain to an endless onion of problems for these folks. Is that the legacy you want to leave behind when our world could easily be described as going to hell in a hand basket? You choose. I pray you choose wisely.

I want to end on a positive note. Once I started forming a positive relationship with God, I attended a process called, "Chazown." "Chazown" is a Hebrew word that means, "purpose." This particular experience was at a local branch of Life.Church. The experience was very neat, and I felt God speaking to me in a very direct way that evening. At the end of it, the idea is you figure out what you are called to do. While I did not know it at the time, I now believe I was called to assemble this book. For the record, my Chazown is "Using my talents to help the suffering overcome." Seems to make sense, doesn't it?

My "Chazown" also came with an accompanying Bible verse that is now my favorite verse: "Not only so, but we also glory in our sufferings, because we know that suffering produces perseverance; perseverance, character; and character, hope." Romans 5:3-4.

My hope for all of you is that you forgive and find peace.

V.

ADDENDUM: LETTERS
TO OFFENDERS

A. LETTER TO DAD

11/7/2019

Dad,

I struggled to write the word "Dad" as you never have been and never will be a father to me. I had a father. His name is [my high school debate coach].

You tortured me. Why? All I did was long to please you. I accomplished more than 10 all-star kids could ever dream of doing. Yet it was never enough for you. Selleraja.

Here is a non-exhaustive list of all the wrongs you did to me:

1. Threatening to kick me out of your home my 17th birthday for trying to pass someone on the highway.
2. The time you broke the kitchen table yelling at [my brother]. I have anxiety and PTSD. Thanks.

3. The time you yelled at me for not properly driving Grandma June's car in the snow when it was stuck. I was 12.
4. The time I was helping you at work and got the forklift stuck. You yelled (shocker) and said, "This is what we call a F*** up!". The only F*** up is you.
5. The time you begged me to move in with you, used money to lure me, and then never came home. You used me only so you wouldn't have to pay [Mom] child support.
6. When I earned a full academic scholarship to a major four-year university, your response was, "That's great, but you're gonna get more, right?"
7. In 7th grade, I earned the Daughters of the American Revolution citizenship award. You skipped the ceremony even though you had notice. [Someone] took me by the shoulder so I felt included. You can thank him one day.
8. The time you came home from the grocery store and [my brother] was too lazy to put soda pop in the fridge. You screamed and threw things. I was so scared I ran outside. PTSD.
9. The time you used the pastor of my church to get out of going to Iraq because you didn't want to pay [Mom] child support. You are a disgrace to your country. When you die, I will make sure the military knows what you did.
10. Your porn addiction. First off, you're a dumb ass because you can get all you want on the internet for free. Second, you're a piece of shit because you would buy porn before you would put food on the table.
11. Always late. How did you make it in the military? That's right, you didn't. You cussed out a Colonel after you lost your temper and got your stripes taken away. Pathetic.
12. The time I found out you were in debt up to your eyeballs. You put my name on your credit cards without my consent or permission. My credit score was damaged when I was trying to buy a home. Thanks.

13. The day [Mom] told you she was leaving you and confessed her credit card problems to you. I can still remember the screams as I was sitting on my swing set. I later learned Aunt Mary had to push you to physically block you from hitting Mom. If I was physically the size then that I am today, would I have beaten you until dental records could not properly identify your corpse. You are very, VERY lucky.

14. Your enabling of [my brother]. God, where to begin. My brother is the physical embodiment of what your style of parenting produces. A convicted felon of 37 years addicted to meth who is unemployed living in his father's basement. A job well done.

15. The way you used me as a trophy to all your friends and workers. You even boasted to them, "Look what I've done." You did nothing. You are not the reason for my success. If anything, you are a hindrance to it.

16. When I begged you for a computer for school, you yelled at me in the middle of Subway and told me, "You have ridden me like a f***ing bicycle." You then told me, "I'll be waiting in the truck." You then stormed out of the restaurant like a two-year-old. Even though I had done nothing wrong, I called you that evening at work (shocker there). I apologized. You responded, "You'll learn." I was 13.

17. When I first moved back in with you, you promised you would be home more. I remember calling you one night and begging you to come home. You didn't come home until midnight.

18. Letting [my brother] call me bladder boy.

19. Buying [my brother] more school clothes than me.

20. The time I had a debate tournament in Joplin. I thought I missed the bus. You drove me to Joplin. I forgot I had the wrong time. You screamed at me. After you dropped me off at the high school, you peeled out of the parking lot. I was so embarrassed I wanted to die.

21. The time you gave me $35.00 for my 12ᵗʰ birthday. I had to ask for more for a bicycle I wanted. You made me feel like shit for asking for $65 for my bday. You even held the check up and said, "Know how much I got for my birthday as a kid?" I shook my head no. You covered the 6 with your finger. I felt so awful I did not want the bike anymore.

22. The Christmas time when I bought you two pairs of sweatpants and a sweater. I was 14 or 15. I saved up my allowance money for 3-4 weeks so I could buy you that. You complained that it wasn't enough. Your exact words, "Two pairs of sweatpants and a sweater for Christmas? Merry Christmas and Happy F***ing new year."

23. The time I got a special gear shifting knob for my first car. I couldn't wait to put it on. You were late of course. I was trying to help, but you were you and being an ass. You then turned it over to me and said, "okay mechanic, you fix it." I did. With minimal effort. I've never seen you so angry.

24. The time I asked for a snack from Sonic. You were driving slowly, and they closed. I was mad; you, madder. You screamed, cussed, and left the house all because I wanted tater tots.

25. The time your quadricolor broke down. You were ripping hoses out of the gas tank. I asked a question. You yelled, "Now is not the time for 20 questions."

26. My brother. Where to begin. Certainly, he is no brother of mine. He beat me, sexually abused me, and even stole my car (which you then took six months to fix the bright switch).

27. Treating me like an errand boy. No idea why. I was always getting parts for you, ordering dinner, or running some errand for you. I'm not your secretary.

28. The women you hurt. Too many to count.

29. Your disgusting vocabulary. Awful.

30. The time we had dinner at [the businessman's] house. I asked him to invite you because I was concerned for you spiritually. You joked with your friends soon after about driving a piece of shit and parking it in front of his house.
31. The time I wrecked my Blazer. Never once asked if I was ok. You screamed, didn't speak to me for 3 days, and never apologized.

I'm sure there are more offenses to list, but you get the point. I understand why you hated me. Mom lied-she said she was on birth control-she wasn't. My only sincere question to you is why didn't you just stay out of my life? I'm sure I would have longed for my dad, but would have none of the horrific scars from the soul-depth wounds you left behind.

Perhaps the most disturbing part of this letter is this. You. Don't. Even. Care. Much like the junker cars you drive, you are the textbook definition of a piece of shit. Even though you definitely do not deserve it, here goes...

"Heavenly father, we all fall short. Dad did, Definitely. But please forgive him. Dad is a mentally ill, bipolar, workaholic without medication or anyone to love him. If anyone needs, but does not deserve, your grace, it most certainly is Dad. I pray that, after 67 years of being a deeply disturbed individual that your overwhelming grace, love, and peace would overwhelm the darkness inside Dad's heart. I pray for infinite prosperity and peace for the remainder of Dad's days."

I want to end by saying that I'm sorry. As a child and even as an adult, I did everything I knew of to please you and it was nowhere near enough. I'm sorry. It was all that I could do.

Sincerely,
Your Son, Ryan

B. LETTER TO JENNIFER

11/3/19

Jennifer,

I honestly don't know what to say to you. Recently, I got very low and very seriously considered suicide. Thankfully, some very strong believers said some very meaningful prayers and I am better now. When I got better, I realized one of my biggest problems is a failure to forgive. I recently saw a message at Life.Church called, "The Faith to Forgive." Honestly, it hit me like a bullet.

I have prayed very seriously for some very horrific things to happen to you. And I meant it. Every word. I don't think you have any idea how bad you hurt me. Allow me to elaborate. While you deny it, I vividly remember you telling me three things: I tried for years to have a child and couldn't; doctors told me I would have a very hard time getting pregnant; and if you did get pregnant, I would not have to be involved.

Let me back up. My mother lied to my father about being on birth control and I was the result. My father treated me like shit. I was physically, mentally, and sexually abused as a child. I was unwanted, and I knew it. I swore two things as an adult. One, I did not want children of my own. Two, I would never end up in a situation like that. Unfortunately, because of your selfishness, both of those vows are broken.

My first paycheck as a lawyer had a child support lien on it. I made more as an intern. I had to move out of the apartment I loved and live in the ghetto where the TPD gang unit routinely patrolled. You prosecuted all arrearage claims, never let me claim [our daughter] on my taxes, and have unreported income through your t-shirt business that causes me to have to pay more. The average obligor has to pay approximately $70k in child support. I will have to pay almost one quarter of a million dollars. Yet none of this seems to phase you. This evidenced by your e-mail where you said you <u>ONLY</u> got $750.00 in child support a month. When it comes to money, you are a fool.

I have shared with a few select friends what you did to me. All are appalled. Most wanted to harm you. A few actually had specific ideas in mind. I stopped them. Although I once wanted you to be harmed, I did not want to upset our daughter.

This letter might seem harsh. Honestly, I don't think it is harsh enough. If this were a contract dispute, I could sue you for fraud in the inducement and collect punitive damages. You would have to pay me. Boy, that would be the day.

Honestly, you don't deserve my forgiveness. Thankfully, that doesn't matter. I have sinned and been forgiven. I did not deserve that. But, I also deserve to be free. Free from the pain you caused, the vows you broke, the sense of betrayal, and the money you have stolen/continue to steal.

I did not think my life could get any worse than my childhood. Then I met you.

Writing this letter, and asking for God's hand on the pen, has been and may always be one of the hardest things I've ever done. Nonetheless, here goes:

"Heavenly Father, I have sinned and received God's grace. By the power given to me by the Holy Spirit, I declare to you and the world that I forgive Jennifer, whether she believes she committed any wrong. I pray your infinite blessings in her life that she may prosper spiritually, financially, and personally. Thank you for sending [the husband of the married couple] into [our daughter's] life to be the father I could not. Thank you for blessing me with a good mind and a strong work ethic so that I can be a generous provider to Jennifer and [our daughter]. I pray the support I give allows [our daughter] to have the childhood I/many only dream of. I pray your spiritual comfort, strength, and grace over

Jennifer, [our daughter], and me. Thank you for sending the Holy Spirit to all of us so we may know forgiveness, and, most importantly, freedom."

I pray your best days are yet to come.

Sincerely,
Ryan

P.S. One of my blessings in life is <u>not</u> good handwriting. Sorry about that.

CPSIA information can be obtained
at www.ICGtesting.com
Printed in the USA
LVHW050449230520
656341LV00003B/487